The Underground Credit Builder's Handbook

What You Need to Know to Build Personal and Business Credit Successfully

Other books by Fourth Dimension

The Seven Ways to Overcome the Federal Statute of Limitations

The Underground Credit Builder's Handbook

What You Need to Know to Build Personal and Business Credit Successfully

By Fourth Dimension

ISBN: 978-0-9980609-0-3

Book design: Dean Fetzer, www.gunboss.com

Cover design: Gary McCluskey,
www.garymccluskey.carbonmade.com

Contents

Introduction

Hello reader. Thank you for purchasing this book. While you may be thinking to yourself that it is rather small, I can assure you that the information found within it is worth its weight in Gold, Platinum, and Black cards.

I wrote this book to show you how to win at this game of credit, because that's what it is, a big game. So many people are losers at this game because they don't have a clue as to how it is played. And until they know how to play the game they are going to keep on losing.

But not you or me. I am a winner and I wrote this handbook so that you can win too. So let's cut the small talk and get started.

I. BANKING

Important Rules

To be a player in this game you are going to have to learn some basic banking rules. Everyone has their own set of rules to go by, I am going to give you mine.

Rule 1: Learn the language

If you don't understand what is being said to you or what you are agreeing to by signing your name, you have already lost the game. Don't be some ignorant fool when you walk into a bank or access one online. I can assure you that the difference between one single word or decimal-point on a contract or form can cost you big bucks. So, as a favor to you, I am putting a Glossary at the end of this book for you to study. Be sure that you do. Knowledge is money in this game my friend, and ignorant people lose theirs.

Rule 2: Make a good impression

I know that everyone can't afford a brand new Armani suit fresh out of the store. But you can still dress well. Even if you have to swallow some pride, go to a consignment shop, the Goodwill, or Salvation Army, and buy the nicest dress clothes that you can afford to pay for. If you need to, have them professionally cleaned and then fitted by a tailor. All that anyone is going to see is a well-dressed businessperson.

Next, you have to take care of your hygiene and personal grooming needs. Don't go into a bank expecting to make connections and be taken seriously when you look and smell like a slob. Iron your clothes, bathe, comb your hair, brush your teeth, trim your nails, and stiffen your back if you slouch.

Finally, be neat, organized and make a good impression.

If you have an appointment, which you should, be on time. Show up with everything you need, turn your cell phone off and keep it out of sight during the meeting. Be sure to walk with good posture, smile, be polite to all banking staff and introduce yourself properly. A good introduction consists of a greeting with an exchange of names, a firm handshake, a smile and thanks to your host for meeting with you.

The point is to look and act like a professional, because professionals like to do business with other professionals.

Rule 3: Come prepared

You need to know what you want beforehand. You don't want to go all the way to the bank and not be able to see who you need to see because you didn't call and make an appointment first. And you don't want to walk into that bank without a clue as to what you want. Bankers will sense your uncertainty and may use it to take advantage of you by selling you financial products that you don't need or which have nothing to do with your goal.

Rule 4: Don't be in a rush

You want to find banks and bankers to do long-term business with. You want to locate people and services that have your best interests in mind. If you are in a hurry, you might settle for a bad deal or end-up having to deal with people or a service you dislike. So have patience. Take things slow if you need to. Do your research. You can always walk away from an offer.

So find the best kind of situation for you to be in, not the first one you stumble across. And this rule includes the well-known principle of "read the fine print." Don't just take someone's word for what something says. Only a fool signs something that they have not read or don't fully understand. If you need to, tell them that you'd like to take it home so that you can read it more and consult with your spouse or attorney. Because once you sign that baby it's a done deal in most cases.

Bank Employees

Once you know the rules to banking, you need to know who the bank's employees are:

Customer Service Representative
- Helps open accounts
- Explains services
- Answers general questions
- Refers people to others who can help
- Provides written information explaining bank products

Teller
- Deposits money
- Cashes checks
- Answers questions
- Refers people to others who can help

Loan Officer
- Takes applications for loans offered at the bank
- Answers questions
- Provides written information explaining loan products
- Helps people fill out loan applications

Branch Manager
- Supervises the bank's operations that take place at that branch

- Helps fix problems that other bank employees can't solve

Account Verification

When you go to open a bank account you will have to go through a process called account verification. Banks want to verify that you are who you say you are and they want to check and see if you have done any previous banking with them or others in the past.

The bank may review your history using companies such as Telecheck or CheckSystems. They will likely run a credit report as well.

Be prepared to present photo identification such as a driver's license, and other identification such as your Social Security Number (SSN) or Individual Taxpayer Identification Number (ITIN) to verify your identity.

If you are not a U.S. citizen, you may be asked to produce your passport, matricula consular card, or resident alien card (Green Card).

The Four C's

When you are applying for loans, lenders like to look into what is known as the Four C's:

Capacity
- Your job and how long you have worked there.
- The amount of money you earn each month.
- Your monthly expenses.

Capital
- The amount of money you have in checking and savings accounts.
- Whether you own a home.
- If you have any investments, property, or assets.

Character
- If you have had credit in the past.
- Whether you have current credit accounts.
- If you have ever filed for bankruptcy, been sued, or foreclosed.
- Whether you have a history of making late payments.

Collateral
- Whether you have assets to use as security for the loan.

II. PERSONAL CREDIT

Identify Your Goals

Everyone needs or wants something different in this game of credit. So when it comes to wealth and finance we all have different goals. I want you to sit down and figure out what your credit goals are. Do you want something small like a $500-limit unsecured credit card? Or do you want something a bit larger like a $1,000,000 line of credit to start a business with? Maybe you just want to bring your FICO score up so that you can re-finance your home mortgage with a lower interest rate.

Any one of these are realistic and obtainable. I just want you to have a clear goal in mind so you know the direction to move towards. When there's no clear goal in sight people tend to act on impulse with little purpose. And that's not how you win at this game. You win at this game with a strategy. So let me ask you an important question: What is your goal?

How's Your Credit History?

Now that you have considered what your goal is, I need to ask you another question so that we can get started: how's your credit history? In other words, do you have a bad credit history, no credit history, or a good credit history?

Before you answer this question, you need to obtain a recent credit report from each of the three major credit reporting agencies: TransUnion, Experian, and Equifax. You can do this by filling out their forms online (see list of resources in back) or you can use the information in the back of this book to make the request by mail (See Appendix A).

Do not assume that you know what your credit report says. I've seen people who have never applied for any credit at all and were stunned when they got a copy of their credit report showing a very lengthy negative credit history because a so-called friend or family member had been using their name and Social Security Number for years. So the only way to be certain is to actually check with the credit reporting agencies.

What to Do Next

Now that we know what kind of credit history you have we can determine what to do next.

Bad Credit History

A bad credit history is not the end of the world. There are ways to fix it in most cases. You will have to put in some time and effort, and will probably have to pay a percentage of what you owe, but it is necessary.

If you have a bad credit history, please skip forward to the section entitled "Resolving Previous Debt Issues."

No Credit History

A history of no credit is not a bad place to start. While you will have difficulty at first in obtaining unsecured credit, there are steps that you can take to get you there.

If you have no credit history, please skip forward to the section entitled "Secured Line of Credit."

Good Credit History

A good credit history is the starting point of the real credit game. If you want to play in the big leagues you've got to have a good credit history.

If you have a good credit history, please skip forward to the section entitled "Your FICO Score."

Resolving Previous Debt Issues

This part is written for my friends with a bad credit history.

Right now is the time to resolve those negative items on your credit report. You don't want those items to be the reason the bank says "no" when you could have put in some time and effort to have them deleted.

There happens to be many ways to resolve debt issues, the right method just depends on the kind of issue at hand. I will lay down the basics and you can go from there:

Pay the Debt

The first way is the most obvious one, pay the debt in exchange for the item's removal. Just be sure to get everything in writing.

Seven Years Old

If the item is more than seven years old it should have already been removed from your credit report automatically. If it has not been removed then you should inform the credit reporting agency in writing that the debt item needs to be deleted.

Inaccuracy

In many cases there are debt items that are not accurate on a person's credit report. Sometimes it is simply a case of mistaken identity, sometimes the debt has already been resolved, and a lot of times someone has perpetrated a fraud under your name and/or Social Security Number. In this kind of situation you would use a Dispute Letter (See Appendix B) to demand removal of the item from your credit report.

Many times there will be a court-awarded judgment against you that you are completely unaware of because you were never "served" (notified). In this circumstance you would file a motion with that court to set-aside/vacate the judgment against you (See Appendix C).

Questionable Debt

If the debt is questionable, you will need to find out who holds the debt "now." While you may have done business with one company and created the debt with them, they may have sold it to another company, a type of collection agency or bank who subsequently made a claim against you and put the negative item on your credit report. In this circumstance you should send this new company a letter demanding proof of the debt and the identity of the original creditor (See Appendix B). If the company does not give you this proof and the identity of the original creditor within 30 days you have the right to demand that the item be removed from your credit report.

If the company is a legit holder of the debt, then you will have to negotiate with them. Most of the time, the debt can be settled for pennies on the dollar. For instance, let's say that you owe $10,000. You would call the company and tell the agent that you are flat broke, your health is bad, you have no assets, and you aren't working, but, you have $800 to give them if they will settle your account, otherwise you are just going to file for bankruptcy protection and then they won't get anything. The odds are with you that they will say yes to your terms.

However, do not give them the money first. Make them send you a written settlement offer in the mail. This offer needs to include the relevant account number along with the signature of the owner or manager of that company. Be sure that the offer states that your debt will be considered as "paid in full" once you pay the agreed upon price. Then, once you have the offer in hand, purchase a cashier's check for that amount and put it in the mail stapled to a copy of the offer along with a letter from you accepting their terms. You must keep copies of all of these documents.

Do not use your personal check, online account, credit or debit cards, or any type of personal financial instrument to pay this settlement with. These people are dirty: they have been known to electronically access people's personal accounts and take the full amount instead of the agreed upon settlement amount. So do like I say, go down to the bank and purchase a cashier's check for that amount.

Once you have successfully dealt with your previous debt items, send the relevant credit reporting agency a letter notifying them of the change if the creditor has not already done so. You have a right to a free corrected credit report, so be sure to send the credit reporting agency a letter demanding a corrected credit report (See Appendix B).

After you have resolved all of your previous debt issues, you should be in a situation almost identical to a person with no credit history. So please skip forward to the section entitled "Secured Line of Credit."

Secured Line of Credit

This part and the following part entitled "Piggybacking" are written for my friends who either don't have a credit history, or, just finished cleaning up a bad one.

Right now no one really wants to give you any unsecured credit. The reason being they don't know whether you can be trusted to pay your bills on time. So you have to find a way to show them that you can be trusted. What is a good way to do this? Answer: obtain a secured line of credit and show a pattern of consistency and dependability by paying your bills on time.

A "secured" line of credit is where you give the creditor something of value to hold on to as a guarantee (usually cash). Based on this guarantee you receive a line of credit. If you use the credit but don't pay back what you owe the creditor keeps the guarantee (also known as "security" hence "secured line of credit").

Typically a secured line of credit comes in the form of a credit card. A secured credit card works like this: let's say that you only have $500 to start out with. You would find a bank that offers secured credit cards and would get the highest one you could with your money. You may have to pay some fees, so let's say that you got offered a $450 secured credit card with a $50 sign up fee. What will happen is that your $450 will go in to an interest-earning savings account for collateral, the bank will keep the other $50 for the fee, and you will be issued a credit card with a $450 limit. Most likely you will have to agree to keep the original $450 in that savings account for a year.

In essence, the bank is lending you your own money when you use the credit card. Just like a regular credit card, you will have to pay interest and late fees and your transactions will be reported to the credit reporting agencies.

After about seven months of using the secured credit card regularly and paying the bill on time, you should be able to find a bank or company online that will issue an unsecured card. And, after the year is up, you can ask your first bank to release your original $450 along with any accumulated interest and ask them to issue you an unsecured credit card also.

Piggybacking

This part – and the previous part entitled "Secured Line of Credit" – is written for my friends who either don't have a credit history, or have just finished cleaning up a bad one.

While a secured line of credit is a great way to get started and get a good credit history going, there's more you can do to really get it going better.

"Piggybacking" is usually referred to when a person jumps on someone's back and has them carry them around. It basically means the same thing in the credit game.

When you are just starting out, you don't have much good credit history, if any at all. So you have to be creative in the ways that will help you build your credit. And since you probably don't have a lot of working capital yet, you have to figure out inexpensive ways to add positive items to your credit history and boost your credit score.

One of the best ways to do this is to find someone with good credit (a FICO score higher than 680 will work for the time being) and have them add you to their bills and/or become an "authorized user" on their credit cards. We call this "piggybacking" because when you do this you are riding on someone else's good credit to benefit your credit status.

The way it works is like this: Let's say that you have a friend with a premium credit score (a FICO score of 720 or more), who has an unsecured credit card with a $25,000 limit. What you do is ask him to call the credit company and put you on the account as an "authorized user." This way, every time he makes purchases and then pays off those purchases you'll get the benefit of it because the credit card company reports the transactions to the credit reporting agencies under both of your names and Social Security Numbers. This is one of the easiest and fastest ways to build your credit and it costs you nothing.

Now let me make something clear about piggybacking before you try it. It is risky to do this. Because if you piggyback with someone who doesn't pay their bill it could reflect negatively on your credit report. So make sure that if you do use this trick you use it with someone who is going to pay their bill. And don't do this trick forever, use it to get your own credit history going and then quit piggybacking.

Your FICO Score

This part and the next part entitled "Start up Capital" are written for all of my friends no matter what their credit history is like.

There's a company called "Fair Isaac Corp." based in San Jose, California.

They developed a system that basically quantifies the likelihood that a borrower will repay money loaned to him or her on time. This system is known as the "FICO score." The higher your FICO score, the more you will see credit opportunities come your way; the lower your FICO score, the less credit opportunities you'll see.

Your FICO score is usually the first thing that most lenders look at. The lowest possible score is 300 and the highest possible score is 850.

The average FICO score is around 692. Most lenders consider people with FICO scores of at least 720 to be prime borrowers.

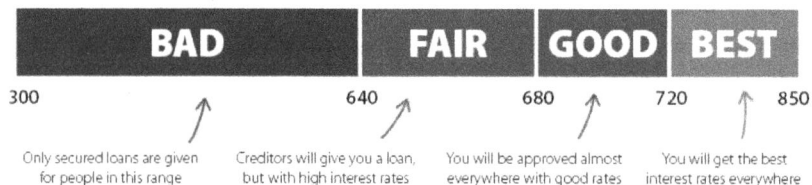

BAD	FAIR	GOOD	BEST

300	640	680	720	850
Only secured loans are given for people in this range	Creditors will give you a loan, but with high interest rates	You will be approved almost everywhere with good rates	You will get the best interest rates everywhere	

To win at this game you must understand how FICO scores are calculated. There are five main factors that go into a FICO score:

1. **Payment History** – Your payment history is the most important factor because it accounts for 35% of your score. To keep this part high simply pay your bills on time.

2. **Overall Amount Owed** – The overall amount you owe is the second biggest factor because it accounts for 30% of the score. This factor pays a lot of attention to how much you owe entirely and how close you are to your credit limits. The bottom line is that they don't like it when you are close to your credit limits.

3. **Extent of Credit History** – The extent of your credit history accounts for 15% of the score. This factor looks hard at the length of your credit history and really favors people with a long track history, say five years or more.

4. **Credit Diversity** – Your credit diversity accounts for 10% of the score. This factor likes to see that you are capable of managing different types of debt rather than just one type.

5. **Recent Credit Applications** – Your recent credit applications account for the remaining 10% of the score. This factor does not like to see multiple recent credit applications and credit inquiries.

Now that you know how your FICO score is calculated, let me give you some tips on how to boost it:

- **Debt-to-Limit** – The most common trick is called the "debt-to-limit" ratio. This is the percentage of your credit line you allow yourself to use. If you want a FICO score of 800 or higher then you had better aim for less than 10%. This means that if you have a credit line of $100,000 you never use more than $10,000 of it before you pay it off. But for the people who are just starting out and don't have a chance of that high a score for a while, I'd say that a 30% debt-to-limit ratio is excellent for the time being. So if you have a credit card with a $1,000 limit on it you would not want to use more than $300 of it before paying it off.

- **Pay Quick** – Another well known strategy is to pay the lender quickly. Most people with credit scores above 750 pay their bills in-full within a week of incurring them. This is where online payments can come in handy as they are usually processed in one to three days.
- **Less is More** – Sometimes you need to know what not to do. For instance, FICO penalizes people who have too many credit cards with balances. The trick is to choose the top two or three cards with the highest spending limits to keep.

Start-up Capital

This part is written for my friends with a good credit history and a good credit score.

It doesn't matter how you raise your start-up capital, but to be a winner in this game you're going to need it. So work hard and save your money, pawn your TV, sell your car, do some odd jobs around the neighborhood or whatever else you've got to do just get it together so that we can get you started.

Here's a rough guideline of what kind of money you'll need to get started:

Your Credit Line Goal	The Start-up Capital
$1,000,000	$250,000
$500,000	$125,000
$100,000	$25,000
$10,000	$2,500

This chart is based on 12-month goals.

While these goals can be done with less or more start-up capital, I advise you to have at least these amounts to begin with along with a good credit history and good FICO score.

As you can see, I use a 25% ratio. In my game plan you'll have 25% of your credit line goal in start-up capital.

Please choose your credit line goal and obtain the start-up capital that corresponds with that goal. Once you have done this, please skip forward to the section entitled "25 Steps of Leverage."

25 Steps of Leverage

This part is written for my friends with a good credit history, a good FICO score, who have identified their credit line goal, and who have obtained the start-up capital amount that corresponds with that goal.

There are many ways to use leverage to get what you want. I am going to give you step-by-step instructions on how to use it to obtain your credit line goal within 12 months. You can use my method, or you can modify it to create your own, it's up to you.

Note: For explanatory purposes I will assume that your credit line goal is $100,000. Whether it is higher or lower, the system stays the same, you'll just adjust amount.

Step 1 – You must have 25% of your credit line goal in start-up capital. Since your goal is $100,000 you must have $25,000 ready. This $25,000 is your start-up capital.

Step 2 – Please select four different banks to do your business with. We will call them "Bank A," "Bank B," "Bank C," and "Bank D."

Step 3 – Go to "Bank A" and open an interest-earning savings account with 40% of your start-up capital. In this case, that would be $10,000, which leaves you with 60% ($15,000) in your pocket which you will need later.

Step 4 – Wait about 10 business days.

Step 5 – Go back to "Bank A" and apply for a 1-year loan for the same amount as what is in your savings account there ($10,000) using your money in that savings account as collateral for the loan.

Step 6 – Take the money borrowed from "Bank A" ($10,000) to "Bank B" and use it to open an interest-earning savings account.

Step 7 – Wait another 10 business days.
Note: The other 60% of your start-up money is for taking care of fees and payments of the loans as they come in. Do not pay more than the minimum payment on the loans, you will be taking out more loans. Also, make sure that there's no penalties for paying the loans off early.

Step 8 – Go back to "Bank B" and apply for a 1-year loan for the same amount as in your savings account ($10,000) and use that money in your savings account as the collateral for the loan.

Step 9 – Take the money borrowed from "Bank B" ($10,000) to "Bank C" and use it to open an interest-earning savings account.

Step 10 – Wait another 10 business days.

Step 11 – Go back to "Bank C" and apply for a 1-year loan for the same amount as in your savings account ($10,000) and use that money in your savings account as collateral for the loan.

Step 12 – Take the borrowed money from "Bank C" ($10,000) and also whatever is left from the other 60% of your start-up money ($15,000 minus fees and payments) to "Bank D" and use it to open an interest-earning savings account.

Step 13 – Make payments to "Bank A," "Bank B," and "Bank C" from "Bank D." Have your payments transferred 5 business days early.

Step 14 – After you have been paying on your loan at "Bank A" for at least 3 months, using funds from "Bank D," you will go into "Bank A" and pay off your first loan in full and then transfer the money out of your savings account there ($10,000 plus interest) into "Bank D."

Step 15 – After you have been paying on your loan at "Bank B" for at least 3 months, using funds from "Bank D," you will go into "Bank B" and pay off your loan there in full and then transfer the money out of your savings account there ($10,000 plus interest) into "Bank D."

Step 16 – After you have been paying on your loan at "Bank C" for at least 3 months, using funds from "Bank D," you will go into "Bank C" and pay off your loan there in full and then transfer the money out of your savings account there ($10,000 plus interest) into "Bank D."

Step 17 – Between step one and fourteen, you should compile a list of credit cards you wish to apply for. Depending on the type of cards and credit limits offered this will determine how many you will choose. Here you will choose five cards with credit limits each valued at least 25% of your credit limit goal. Assuming your credit limit goal is $100,000, you will choose five cards each with credit limits of $25,000 and higher. Note: At this point you should already have great credit: all of your loans should be paid off in full and you should have at least 40% of your start-up money ($10,000) sitting in "Bank D."

Step 18 – Obtain credit card applications from each of the banks/companies offering the cards you wish to apply for.

Step 19 – When you receive the applications, fill in the information using your Banks "A," "B," and "C" as reference and list the money in "Bank D" ($10,000 plus) as a liquid asset (but not for collateral). In many cases the credit score won't even be checked where someone has listed three banks for reference.

Step 20 – Complete all credit card applications, but do not mail them off yet. First, make appointments with Banks "A," "B," and "C" to come in and apply for loans.

Step 21 – Go to each of your bank appointments (Banks "A," "B," and "C") and apply for unsecured loans in the highest amounts available. Do not use your money in "Bank D" as security. The very least you should get from each bank is 100% of what you initially deposited and loaned against and repaid ($10,000 in this case). This should bring you to 30% of your credit line goal.

Step 22 – Next, go to "Bank D" and ask for two loans:, one unsecured loan for 10% of your credit line goal ($10,000), and the other one a secured loan using the money in the savings account there as collateral ($10,000 plus) for another 10% of your credit line goal ($10,000). This, in conjunction with step 21, should bring you to 50% of your credit line goal.

Step 23 – Now that you have your bank loans taken care of, you can mail in your credit card applications. Mail them all at the same time.

Step 24 – Out of the five credit cards you apply for, you only need two to be approved in order to fulfill the other 50% of your credit line goal.

Step 25 – Now that you have met your credit line goal (a total credit amount of $100,000), be sure to use it wisely my friend. And that means to use only what you need.

It is assumed that you will only utilize the amount of credit available to you that you are capable of making payments on. The goal of this section is to show you how to obtain the credit itself. It is beyond the scope of this book to show you how to use all your credit and then pay for it. This is something that you must figure out yourself.

Note: Even if you are not approved initially for the full amounts of credit you applied for, you can take what is offered and leverage against it like I have shown you until you meet your goal. Remember, my start-up capital chart is based on a 12-month period. I designed these steps so that you would finish all 25 of them in half that time just in case you have to do more leveraging to reach your goal. No one can say for certain how a bank or credit lending company will act.

The key is to try, try and try again. Don't ever give up on yourself, you can do it. Now get out there and win!

III. BUSINESS CREDIT

Get Started

If you are reading this chapter, you probably either started your own business already or have an idea you'd like to turn into a business. Since it is not possible for me to know which class you fall into, I am going to take it from the start.

The Idea

Every business starts with an idea. Maybe your idea is to do something that has never been done before. Maybe your idea is to make something already existing better. Maybe you want to buy an established business or buy into a franchise. Whatever the case, it all starts with an idea.

Take your idea and write it down. Analyze it. Conduct research on its feasibility. Look for other ideas similar to it and compare yours to theirs.

Once you have decided to make your idea become a reality and are determined to see it through, you have taken the first step to entrepreneurship.

Develop a Business Plan

When successful people do business they usually have a business plan.

I'm not saying that the whole process needs to be rigid and cemented to a paper theory. But a person is wise to figure out the direction they are heading before they start walking. You know what I mean? Give yourself an outline before starting. This will help you be more efficient and productive in your venture and, as a result, increase the likelihood of your ultimate success. So take the time to develop a business plan.

I have put a Business Plan Outline (See Appendix D) in the back of this book for you to use as a reference when developing your business plan.

The Business Entity

After you have figured out what kind of business you want to be in and have developed a business plan, you'll need to select a business entity.

Sole Proprietorship

A "sole proprietorship" is a business owned/operated by an individual who has chosen to not create a legal entity separate from his or her personal liabilities.

In this case, the owner and the business are not legally distinct entities and the individual will be legally and financially liable for all acts of the enterprise.

A proprietor's revenue is described as business income on Schedule C of the IRS 1040 but becomes personal income unless it is reduced by direct expenses for producing the revenue.

Partnership

A "partnership" is the legal relation existing between two or more individuals or legal entities that have chosen to structure their business in a registered partnership.

Partnerships are typically defined as "general" or "limited."

A general partnership is one that divides the responsibility and liabilities among the partners.

A limited partnership is one that limits the responsibility and/or liability among the partners.

A partnership's revenue is taxed by dividing both the profits and losses among the partners as agreed upon.

C Corporation

A "C Corporation" is an organization that is authorized by state law to act as a legal entity separate from its shareholders (owners). As a result, shareholders enjoy limited liability for the debts, obligations and liabilities incurred by the business.

S Corporation

A "S Corporation" is also an organization that is authorized by state law to act as a legal entity separate from its shareholders (owners). The shareholders thus enjoy limited liability for the debts, obligations and liabilities incurred by the business also. The main difference between a C Corporation and a S Corporation is the way that they are taxed.

Unlike a C Corporation, a S Corporation does not itself pay any income taxes. Instead, the shareholders (owners) must report the business income and expenses on their individual tax return, just like those doing business as sole proprietorships, partnerships, and Limited Liability Companies (LLC's).

Limited Liability Company (LLC)

A "Limited Liability Company" is a company in which the investor's potential loss is limited to the amount of their investments in the event that the business fails.

LLC's are popular because they provide a high level of protection from personal liability just like corporations do, and yet still receive the tax benefits of other types of entities.

An LLC can choose to be taxed as a corporation or use the tax structure of proprietorships, partnerships, or corporations.

Employer's Identification Number

If you are starting a business you need a tax identification number also known as an "Employer's Identification Number."

This number will be needed to obtain business credit, even if your business doesn't have employees. And it can be applied for online with the IRS at www.irs.gov, or through the mail at: Internal Revenue Service, 1111 Constitution Avenue, N.W., Washington, D.C. 20224.

The Employer's Identification Number must be tied in with your Social Security Number (SSN), or the SSN of any officer in your corporation. But whoever's SSN is used, be sure that the name of that person is listed on the Officer's List of your corporation.

Business Credit Basics

If you want to get premium business credit in this game then you've got to know the business credit basics.

> D and B Profile and Duns Number – Dun and Bradstreet covers more than two-thirds of the market share for business credit reporting (Experian covers most of the rest). And what they do is create credit profiles on businesses using information provided by the business owners and vendors doing business with the company and issue them "Duns Numbers."

> They also grant a "Paydex Score" to businesses based on payment history and issue a "Duns Rating" based on the financial statements of the business.

Before you contact Dun and Bradstreet for your D and B Profile and Duns Number, be sure that your business has the following:

1. A phone number listed in the business directory of the local phone company.

2. Live operators or employees answering the phone at all times.

3. All required documents filed with your incorporating state, i.e. Articles of Incorporation, Officer's List, etc.

4. Receipts for all corporate filing fees and taxes.

5. An actual brick and mortar location.

6. All required licenses to operate such business.

Paydex Score – Paydex scores range from 0 to 100 with 100 being the highest. And it works by taking into account things like the timeliness of your pay history to vendors.

A good Paydex score is 65 and higher. And it is the businesses that can meet the following criteria that get a good Paydex score:

1. Been in business for at least two to three years.

2. Gross more than $350,000 in sales a year.

3. Have at least ten employees.

4. The business is in the same state as the officer/owner.

A premium Paydex score is 75 and higher. And it is the businesses that can meet the following criteria that get a premium Paydex score:

1. Been in business for at least five years.

2. Gross more than $1 million in sales a year.

3. Have at least 25 employees.

4. The business is in the same state as the officer/owner.

5. Have more than one branch office.

6. Be able to present five different vendors as reference who report directly to Dun and Bradstreet.

It is also good to have a website that shows up in major search engines like Google and Bing.

Need Start-up Capital?

Some people reading this book will probably have difficulty in acquiring the capital they need to start their business with. So as a favor, I am going to share some of the best ways I know to get the money you need to form your business with.

Bootstrapping

When you have plenty of ideas but are short on cash, the solution to your problem may very well be "bootstrapping." Bootstrapping is essentially using creative ways to start a business or enterprise with little overhead and little money out of pocket. The objective here is to drive down the start-up cost and overcome the need for financing. There's really no definitive list of things to do, but some of the more common tricks are to:

- minimize the overhead
- don't pay yourself a salary
- collect the money first then make and deliver the product
- lower the scale of the business launch
- be frugal in your expenses and lifestyle
- find free labor (volunteers)
- have someone pay you to develop the product and then sell it to others

Bartering

When you don't have the money to pay for something outright you may think that it is not obtainable. But there are other ways to acquire goods and services besides paying in cash.

One way that is growing more and more popular is "bartering." Before currency was invented, people bartered. Bartering is simply exchanging goods or services for another's goods or services.

For example, if a professional window-washer needs his pool cleaned, he may be able to trade 2 hours of window washing for 2 hours of pool cleaning from a professional pool cleaner. In fact, there are even barter clubs that help provide an exchange for barters.

It should be pointed out that barter clubs do keep track of transactions and provide an IRS form 1099 for the value of the goods or services bartered.

Crowdsourcing

When you have a service or product that can be marketed to many, "Crowdsourcing" may be a useful to help you get started.

Crowdsourcing is a type of micro-financing. Typically, the entrepreneur pitches the idea to multiple investors, sometimes hundreds or even thousands of people, who will consider the plan, idea, and strategy and then decide whether to make a investment in your company.

In many cases the investments will not be loans but instead take the form of gifts or grants.

One of the most popular and prominent venues for crowdsourcing is found online at: www.kickstarter.com.

Trade Credit

When a company is in the start-up stage it usually doesn't have access to traditional business loans and credit cards. A good way to get access to the goods and services you need at this stage may be in the form of "trade credit."

Trade credit is where you get companies that your business relies on for goods and services to open an account and give you access to those goods and/or services on the basis of a credit line with them.

This will enable you to get your business started without upfront costs or dependence on banks and credit card companies for loans.

Partnerships

If you have tried to bootstrap your start-up and have failed at getting loans, you can always look for a partner.

Getting a partner may be the solution to your problem. Just be sure to choose wisely when you are choosing partners. When you are considering someone for the purpose of a partnership, consider what they will be bringing into the deal with them, including the good, bad and ugly aspects of it all.

The best kind of partner is the one who brings more than just money into the deal: knowledge and skills are worth money in the long run.

Leveraging

When you are having a hard time getting an unsecured loan for your business, you may have to look at getting a secured loan. The basis of a secured loan will be the asset you put up as security against it. This is called "leveraging."

Leveraging is when you use an asset as leverage to gain a loan. Assets come in many forms and a creative-minded person could use all sorts of things as an asset to use as leverage. The typical assets used are financial instruments, home equity, 401(k) accounts, IRA accounts, jewelry, vehicles, land, antique goods, etc. If something is valuable to someone else, it is likely that it can be sold for value or used as an asset.

Government Guaranteed Loans

Many people don't know it, but the U.S. Government has multiple loan guarantee programs for aspiring entrepreneurs to access funds from.

The most popular ones are the U.S. Small Business Administration (SBA), U.S. Department of Agriculture (USDA), and the Export-Import Bank of the United States (Ex-ImBank).

SBA

The Small Business Administration offers loan protection to banks who loan to businesses that meet certain specifications. The two primary loan guarantees programs offered by the SBA are the 504 Loan Program and the 7(a) Loan Program.

The "504 Loan Program" provides small types of businesses access to long-term, fixed-rate loans for things like expansion and modernization. But, the proceeds from the 504 Program loan cannot be used for working capital, inventory, or repaying debt.

The "7(a) Loan Program" provides small types of businesses access to long-term, fixed-rate and variable-rate loans for things like acquisition or improvement of assets, refinancing existing debt, or working capital.

The Small Business Administration also has other loan guarantee programs such as:

- "Community Advantage Program" (for borrowers located in under-served communities)
- "Patriot Express Program" (for veterans or members of the military)
- "The Small/Rural Lender Advantage Program" (for borrowers in rural areas, especially communities experiencing population loss, economic dislocation, and high unemployment)

USDA

The U.S. Department of Agriculture offers loan protection to banks who loan to small business owners in rural areas through its Business and Industry Guarantee Program (B&I).

A rural community is basically an area with a population less than 50,000 people.

Ex-Im Bank

The Export-Import Bank of the United States guarantees payment of U.S. company sales abroad and provides term financing guarantees for foreign companies and countries that are buying American products if other financing is not available locally.

IV. RESOURCES

Glossary

Account Verification

A procedure that lets a bank determine whether people are who they say they are and whether they will be a responsible bank account customer. The banks usually review the customer's banking history by running searches through companies such as TeleCheck or ChexSystem and typically also run a full credit report.

Adjustable-Rate Mortgage (ARM)

An adjustable-rate mortgage has an interest rate that changes periodically according to the cost of the funds to the lender.

Annual Percentage Rate (APR)

The APR is the yearly percentage rate on a loan.

Annual Privacy Notices

The yearly notice financial companies give their customers about its privacy policy.

Asset

An item of value owned.

Attachment

An attachment is a lien against personal property.

Automated Teller Machine (ATM)

A computerized electronic machine that performs basic banking functions such as handling check deposits or issuing cash withdrawals.

Balance

The balance is the amount of money you have in your bank account.

Balance Computation Method

Determines how your interest is calculated.

Balloon Mortgage

A balloon mortgage is one that has a large payment at the end of the loan term.

Bank

An establishment for the custody, loan, exchange, or issue of money, for the extension of credit and for facilitating the transmission of funds.

Bankruptcy

Bankruptcy is a legal declaration of insolvency. Bankruptcy will not fix credit record problems and will be part of a credit history for ten years. A new law now requires that debtors get credit counseling before they can file for bankruptcy.

Branch Manager

A branch manager is the person who supervises the bank operations at that branch and helps fix problems that cannot be solved by other bank workers.

Broker

An agent who negotiates purchases and sales such as real estate, commodities, or securities.

Capacity

Capacity refers to the ability to make timely payments.

Capital

Capital refers to the value of a person's assets and net worth.

Caps

Caps are provisions which limit how much a rate can change at each adjustment period or over the life of the loan.

Car Title

The legal document that indicates the owner of the vehicle.

Character

Character refers to how a person has paid bills or debts in the past. The credit report is one way lenders will assess a person's character.

Checking Account

A checking account is an account that allows a person to write checks to pay bills or buy goods.

Closing Costs

Closing costs are the charges associated with the transfer of property.

Collateral

Collateral is the property or asset that is promised to the lender as security on a loan.

Collection Account

A collection account is a past-due account that has been referred to a specialist to collect part or all of the debt.

Compensation Factors

Compensation factors are favorable factors that might outweigh the negative factors.

Conventional Loan

A conventional loan is a mortgage that is not guaranteed, insured, or made by the Federal Government.

Credit

Financial or commercial trustworthiness.

Credit Report

A credit report is a record of how borrowers have paid their debts.

Credit Union

A non-profit institution owned by people who have something in common.

Customer Service Representative or New Account Officer

The customer service representative is the person who helps customers open their accounts. The representative also explains services, answers general questions, makes referrals to others who can help, and provides written information explaining the bank products.

Debt Management Plan (DMP)

In a DMP, money is deposited each month with a credit counseling organization, which then uses the deposits to pay unsecured debts (such as credit card bills, student loans, and medical bills) according to a payment schedule the counselor develops with the creditors.

Debt-to Income Ratio (DTI)

Debt-to Income Ratio, or DTI, is the ratio of monthly debt payments to monthly gross income. Lenders use DTI ratio to determine whether a borrower's income qualifies him or her for a mortgage.

Deposit

A deposit is the money added to an account.

Dispute Letter

A dispute letter is a letter sent to a credit reporting agency to challenge an error in a credit report. The credit reporting agencies are required to conduct an investigation within 30 days of receiving the letter.

Electronic Fund Transfer Act (EFTA)

The Electronic Fund Transfer Act establishes rights, liabilities, and responsibilities of customers who use electronic fund transfer services and the banks that offer these services.

Equal Credit Opportunity Act (ECOA)

The Equal Credit Opportunity Act (ECOA) protects consumer rights throughout the loan process. ECOA promotes the availability of credit to all credit worthy applicants without regard to race, color, religion, national origin, sex, martial status, age, or receipt of public assistance income, or exercise of rights under the Consumer Credit Protection Act.

Equity

Equity is the value of the home minus the debt, usually in the form of a home loan.

Fair Debt Collection Practices Act (FDCPA)

The Fair Debt Collection Practices Act helps eliminate abusive debt collection practices.

Fair Credit Billing Act (FCBA)

The Fair Credit Billing Act requires creditors to promptly credit payments and correct billing mistakes for open-ended accounts such as credit cards.

Fair Credit Reporting Act (FCRA)

The Fair Credit Reporting Act requires that the lender notify borrowers of the reason they were denied loan or credit. Specifically, if it had something to do with information found in their credit report.

Fees

The sums paid or charged for a service.

FICO score

The FICO score (an acronym for the Fair Isaac Corporation) is the method lenders use to calculate the credit-worthiness of a borrower by comparing the information in credit reports to what is on the credit reports of thousands of other customers. FICO scores range from 300 to 850.

Finance Charge

The total dollar amount a loan cost. Including items such as interest, service charges, and loan fees.

Fixed-Rate Loan

A fixed-rate loan has an interest rate and payment amount that stays the same throughout the term of the loan.

Foreclosure

Foreclosure is a legal proceeding initiated by a creditor to take possession of collateral that secured a defaulted loan.

Government Mortgages

A government mortgage is insured by the government, typically through the Department of Housing and Urban Development (HUD), through the Federal Housing Administration, or guaranteed by the Department of Veterans Affairs or the Rural Housing Service.

Grace Period

The grace period is the number of days a borrower has to pay the balance before a creditor starts charging interest.

Home Equity Loan

Home equity loans are secured by property of the borrower. The amount of equity is the value of the property minus the debt. Home equity loans generally can be used for any reason.

HUD-1 Settlement Statement

A HUD-1 Settlement Statement is a summary of all the costs paid by the buyer and seller in a mortgage transaction.

Index

The index is a base interest used to calculate the interest rate that will be charged on a variable-rate loan. The rate paid on a variable rate loan is usually a set percentage above the base rate, or the index.

Individual Development Account (IDA)

An IDA is a matched savings account. When an account is matched, it means that another organization, such as a foundation, corporation, or government entity, agrees to add money to your account.

Installment Loan

This is a loan that is repaid in equal monthly payments, or installments, for a specific period of time, usually several years.

Interest

Interest is the amount of money financial institutions charge for lending their money.

Judgment

A judgment is a court placing a lien on a debtor's property as security for a debt owed to a creditor. It remains on the credit report for seven years from the date it was filed.

Lien

A lien is a legal claim on property that secures the promise to repay the debt.

Loan Officer

The loan officer is the person who takes applications for loans offered at the bank. The officer can answer questions, provide written information explaining loan products, and help fill out loan applications.

Loan to Value (LTV)

Loan to Value or LTV is the amount of money borrowed compared to the price of the property being purchased.

Mortgage

A mortgage is a legal document whereby the borrower pledges property to the lender to ensure payment of a loan.

Periodic Rate

The periodic rate is an interest rate applied to a balance to calculate the finance charge.

Point

A point is the amount equal to one percent of the loan amount.

Previous Balance

The previous balance is the amount owed at the end of the previous billing period.

Principal

The principal is the loan amount borrowed or still remaining on the loan.

Rate Lock

A rate lock is the time period, usually 30 to 60 days, that a mortgage lender agrees to hold the mortgage rate and points payable by the borrower to the rate quoted by the lender on a given day.

Refund Anticipation Loan

Refund anticipation loans are short-term loans secured by income tax refunds.

Saving Account

A savings account is an account that earns interest. Some banks will give customers a booklet called a "passbook" to keep track of the money.

Secured Loan

A secured loan is one where the borrower offers collateral for the loan.

Subprime Lending

Subprime lending involves extending credit to borrowers who have a higher risk of defaulting on their loans than traditional bank customers because of past problems with credit.

Tax Lien

A tax lien is a claim against property assets filed by the taxing authority for unpaid taxes. It remains on credit reports for seven years.

Teller

The teller is the person behind the counter who takes money, answers questions, cashes checks, or makes referrals to others who can help. Tellers are the main contact people at the bank.

Title

The title indicates the right of ownership in the property.

Truth in Lending Act (TILA)

The Truth in Lending Act or TILA requires lenders to disclose the total cost of a loan, including the finance charge and the annual percentage rate (APR). In addition, it gives consumers the right to cancel certain types of home loans within three days.

Unsecured Loan

An unsecured loan is not backed by collateral. Credit cards are examples of unsecured loans.

Variable Rate Loan

This is a loan that has an interest rate that might change during the period of the loan, as written in the loan agreement or contract.

Withdrawal

A withdrawal is the process of taking money from an account.

Contact Information and Websites

Annual Credit Report Request Service

A place where consumers can submit a report for a free annual credit report from all three of the major credit reporting bureaus (Equifax, Experian, and Trans Union).

You can write to this address to request the free form:

Annual Credit Report Request Service
P.O. Box 105281
Atlanta, GA 30348-5281

Or, you can go online and print out a copy of the form:

www.annualcreditreport.com or www.ftc.gov/credit

Association of Independent Consumer Credit Counseling Agencies (AICCCA)

A national membership organization that promotes quality and consistency in the delivery of credit counseling services.

You can visit them online for more information at:

wmv.aiccca.org

Or you can reach them on the phone at:

800-450-1794

Dun & Bradstreet

Covers more than two-thirds of the market share for business credit reporting. They also issue them "Duns Numbers."

You can visit them online for more information at:

www.dnb.com

Or you can reach them on the phone at:

973-921-5500

Equifax

One of the major credit reporting bureaus that lenders use to help make their decisions as whether to give consumers credit or not.

To order a credit report:

Equifax
P.O. Box 740241
Atlanta, GA 30374-0241
800-685-1111

To report credit fraud:

Equifax
P.O. Box 740241
Atlanta, GA 30374-0241
800-525-6285

Experian

One of the major credit reporting bureaus that lenders use to help make their decisions as whether to give consumers credit or not.

To order a credit report:

Experian
P.O. Box 2002
Allen, TX 75013
888-397-3742

To report credit fraud:

Experian
P.O. Box 9530

Allen, TX 75013

888-397-3742

FederalConsumer Information Center (FCIC)

Provides free online consumer information to help the public and produces the Consumer Action Handbook which is designed to help citizens find the very best sources for assistance with their consumer problems and questions.

You can visit them online for more information at:

www.pueblo.gsa.gov

Or you can reach them on the phone at:

800-688-9889

First Gov

The official online gateway to all government information and services. If you are not sure as to what government service or agency you are in need of you should start your inquiry here.

You can visit them online for more information at:

www.firstgov.gov

Go Direct

Offers sign up for the direct depositing of Social Security or Supplemental Income payments.

You can visit them online for more information at:

www.godirect.org

Or you can reach them on the phone at:

800-333-1795

Kickstarter

A web venue where entrepreneurs can pitch their idea or request to potential investors for crowdfunding.

You can visit them online for more information at:

www.kickstarter.com

My Money

The government's website dedicated to teaching Americans about finance.

You can visit them online for more information at:

www.mymoney.gov

The National Association of Government Guaranteed Lenders (NAGGL)

The National Association of Government Guaranteed Lenders, or NAGGL, is an association of banks and lenders that offer SBA loans.

You can visit them online for more information at:

www.naggl.org

Or you can reach them on the phone at:

405-377-4022

National Foundation for Credit Counseling

A national non-profit organization that helps people resolve credit problems.

You can visit them online for more information at:

www.nfc.org

Or you can reach them on the phone at:

800-388-2227

Practical Money Skills

A website that offers tools and information about credit, finance, and so forth.

You can visit them online for more information at:

www.practicalmoneyskills.com

Trans Union

One of the major credit reporting bureaus that lenders use to help make their decisions as to whether to give consumers credit or not.

To order a credit report:

Trans Union
P.O. Box 1000
Chester, PA 19022
800-888-4213

To report credit fraud:

Trans Union
P.O. Box 6790
Fullerton, CA 92634
800-680-7289

What's My Score

A website that offers a consumer credit score estimator.

You can visit them for more information at:

www.whatsmyscore.org/estimator

APPENDIX A
Free Annual Credit Report

Free Annual Credit Report

Thanks to the Fair and Accurate Transactions Act of 2003 (FACT Act), consumers are entitled to a free credit report disclosure every 12 months from each of the national/major credit reporting agencies. By law, the consumer's request for a credit report will be processed within 15 days of its receipt.

The easiest and most effective way to get your free annual credit report is to fill out the Annual Credit Report Request Form and mail it back to them.

You can write to this address to request the free form:

Annual Credit Report Request Service
P.O. Box 105281
Atlanta, GA 30348-5281

Or, you can go online and print out a copy of the form:

www.annualcreditreport.com or www.ftc.gov/credit

It should be noted that credit file disclosures can be requested and then viewed instantly on the website. If you have a printer, they can be printed directly from this website, too.

APPENDIX B
Sample Dispute Letters

To: _____   Date   _____

_____

Certified Mail
Number   _____

_____

Social Security
Number   _____

From: _____

Account
number   _____

_____

Date of Birth   _____

Formal Dispute Letter to Credit Bureau

Re: _____

(inaccurate item)

Dear Sir/Madam,

Your company is reporting an inaccurate item that I have listed above on my credit report. There is no basis for this item to be on my credit report, it is not a legitimate item and I am therefore formally requesting that it be deleted/removed at once.

This inaccuracy is completely unacceptable and is interfering with my credit and finances. Please consider this to be my formal Dispute Letter under provisions of the Fair Credit Reporting Act, the Fair Debt Collection Practices Act, and the Fair Credit Billing Act. Please be aware that I am invoking the protections and rights of these laws and all other laws applicable.

Please note that under federal law you have 30 days from the receipt of this letter to complete your reinvestigation. 15 U.S.C. § 1681i(a)(1).

If there is any document or form that I need to sign in order to confirm that this reported item is inaccurate, please mail it to me within this 30 day period so that I can indeed sign it. This item is not accurate whatsoever.

Moreover, I hereby request that you send me a detailed description of the procedure and steps you took to determine the accuracy of this item within 15 days of the completion of your reinvestigation.

Signature _____

To: _____   Date _____

_____   Certified Mail
Number _____

_____   Social Security
Number _____

From: _____   Account
number _____

_____   Date of Birth _____

Corrected Credit Report from Credit Bureau

Re: _____

(previously disputed item)

Dear Sir/Madam,

More than 30 days ago I sent to you a formal Dispute Letter challenging the above listed item on my credit report as inaccurate. That Dispute Letter was sent and received by you via Certified Mail which I tracked using the U.S. Postal Service's website. You had 30 days from the receipt of my Dispute Letter to conduct and finish your reinvestigation into the accuracy of this challenged item. The time to investigate/reinvestigate has expired. This time limit is a statutory limit prescribed by law. 15 U.S.C. § 1681i(a)(1).

This debt item is not a legitimate one and it is causing me emotional distress and is interfering with my credit and finances. Please consider this to be my formal letter to you demanding a corrected credit report showing me proof that you have deleted/removed this above listed item from my credit report as you are required to do so under the law. 15 U.S.C. § 1681s-2(b)(2) and 1681i(a)(1)(A). And, I demand that the envelope containing this corrected credit report be post-marked within 5 days of the receipt of this letter.

Please note, if I do not receive an updated credit report showing that the above listed item has been removed/deleted, my attorney will be filing suit shortly as to your negligent and willful noncompliance with the law.

Signature _____

CC: Federal Trade Commission; Consumer Protection Agency; Department of Business and Professional Regulations; Subcommittee on Banking, Credit, and Insurance

To: _____   Date _____

_____

Certified Mail
Number _____

_____

Social Security
Number _____

From: _____

Account
number _____

_____

Date of Birth _____

_____

Notice to Credit Bureau of Intent to File Complaint

Re: _____

(previously disputed item)

Dear Sir/Madam,

You shall consider this letter as my formal "Notice of Intent to File a Complaint with the Federal Trade Commission."

As you have already been made aware, the above listed item on my credit report is inaccurate. This inaccuracy is unacceptable and is interfering with my credit and finances.

Your time to investigate/reinvestigate has expired and you are now in both negligent and willful noncompliance under federal law. As you know, you can be held liable under the law and if you do not immediately remove this item from my credit report I will seek redress in federal court. See, e.g. Wenger v. Trans Union

<u>Corp.</u>, No. 95-6445 (C. Dist. CA 1995); and, 15 U.S.C. §§ 41 and 1681 et seq.

You are further requested to notify all creditors of this inaccuracy who had received a copy of my credit report with this disputed item on it in the last 6 months.

Signature _____

CC: Federal Trade Commission; Consumer Protection Agency; Department of Business and Professional Regulations; and, Subcommittee on Banking, Credit, and Insurance

To: _____   Date _____

_____

_____   Certified Mail
Number _____

_____   Social Security
Number _____

From: _____   Account
number _____

_____

_____   Date of Birth _____

Potential Bankruptcy Letter to Creditor

Re: _____

(type of debt and debt amount)

Dear Sir/Madam,

For several years now my family and I have been hit with a number of financial and health problems. These problems have caused me to be unable to make good on my debt to you.

Believe me, it is not that I don't want to settle this debt with you, because I do. The problem is that I cannot afford to pay this amount. I would like nothing more than to pay you and be done with it. But I just don't have the money to do so.

Recently, I have decided to look into filing for bankruptcy protection. My friends and family do not want me to do this and have offered to give me some money to settle this debt with you to prevent me from filing bankruptcy. As a result of their kindness, I can offer you the following amount to settle this debt:

$ _____

While I know that this is only a small amount of what I owe, it is all that I can come up with. If you would like this amount rather than nothing at all, please have the owner or manager send me a formal letter offering to settle my debt in full for this amount. If you do this, I will send you a letter back accepting your offer along with a cashier's check for this amount. If not, please cease all further communication with me.

Signature _____

To: _____   Date _____

_____

Certified Mail
Number _____

_____

Social Security
Number _____

From: _____

Account
number _____

_____

Date of Birth _____

Formal Dispute Letter to Alleged Creditor

Re: _____

(inaccurate item)

Dear Sir/Madam,

Your company is currently reporting a negative listing to one or all of the major credit reporting bureaus (Experian, Trans Union, and Equifax) in regards to the above-numbered account. I have gone through my personal records and have thus concluded that there is no reason for you to report such items on my credit report. If you will please review your records and reinvestigate this matter you will see that there has been an error.

This inaccuracy is completely unacceptable and is interfering with my credit and finances. Please consider this to be my formal Dispute Letter under provisions of the Fair Credit Reporting Act, the Fair Debt Collection Practices Act, and the Fair Credit Billing Act. Please be aware that I am invoking the protections and rights of these laws and all other laws applicable.

Please note that under federal law you have 30 days from the receipt of this letter to complete your reinvestigation.

If there is any document or form that I need to sign in order to confirm that this reported item is inaccurate, please mail it within this 30 day period so that I can indeed sign it. This item is not accurate and I am hereby asking that it be removed/deleted accordingly.

I request that you send me a description of the procedure you used to determine the accuracy of this item within 15 days of the completion of your reinvestigation.

Signature _____

To:	_____	Date	_____
	_____		
	_____	Certified Mail Number	_____
	_____	Social Security Number	_____
From:	_____		
	_____	Account number	_____
	_____		
	_____	Date of Birth	_____

Inquiry Removal Request to Inquirer

Re: _____

(date of unauthorized inquiry)

Dear Sir/Madam,

According to my most recent credit report, your company is reporting to one or all of the major credit reporting bureaus (Experian, Trans Union, and Equifax) that I applied to you for credit.

I did not grant you permission to review/make inquiry into my credit report. The Fair Credit Reporting Act (15 U.S.C. § 1681, et seq.) requires that a creditor be able to verify the written authorization of the consumer giving the creditor permission to review their credit.

If you can provide a copy of the credit application or letter that I personally signed showing where I have authorized the disclosure of my credit file to you, I will accept the inquiry on my credit report as a legitimate one. If you cannot provide me with a written authorization signed by me granting you authorization then you are required by law to remove the inquiry from the credit reporting bureaus.

Please note that the existence of this unauthorized credit inquiry on my credit report is having an adverse effect on my ability to obtain credit. Time is thus of the essence and I look forward to receiving proof of authorization for this inquiry or proof that you have had it removed from my credit report within 30 days.

Be advised, I am invoking and preserving my rights under the law and if you refuse to act in a timely fashion my attorney will be filing suit very shortly as to your negligent and willful noncompliance with the law.

Signature _____

To: _____   Date _____

_____

Certified Mail
Number _____

_____

Social Security
Number _____

From: _____

Account
number _____

_____

Date of Birth _____

_____

Formal Dispute Letter to Collection Agency

Re: _____

(inaccurate item)

Dear Sir/Madam,

Your company is attempting to collect a debt from me that I did not create nor am I responsible for. You have made negative reports to one or more of the major credit reporting bureaus (Experian, Trans Union, and Equifax) about me and have been attempting to communicate with me at unusual times and places about this inaccurate debt item listed above.

I do not know you. I did not do business with you. I do not owe you any money. The items you have placed on my credit report are inaccurate. Please consider this my formal Dispute Letter to you disputing the above listed item.

I am invoking my rights and protections under the provisions of the Fair Credit Reporting Act, the Fair Debt Collection Practices Act, and the Fair Credit Billing Act.

I hereby request the following: the identity of the original creditor; proof of the debt; a copy of the contract, document, or instrument bearing my signature; evidence of your authorization under 15 U.S.C. § 1692(e) and 15 U.S.C. § 1692(f) in this alleged matter; proof of your authorization of law to collect and possess my personal financial information; evidence of your authorization to do business or operate in this state; the name, address, and phone number of the person who you obtained my name and social security number from. Please be advised that you have 30 days from the date you have received this letter to comply with my request. I am tracking this letter via the U.S. Postal Service certified mail service and will enforce my rights and protections under the law without delay.

Signature _____

To: _____   Date _____

_____

Certified Mail
Number _____

_____

Social Security
Number _____

From: _____

Account
number _____

_____

Date of Birth _____

Cease Communication Letter to Collection Service

Re: _____

(type of debt and debt amount)

Dear Sir/Madam,

For more than 90 days now, I have received letters and phone calls from your company concerning the above listed debt item.

As I have informed you time after time, I cannot pay this bill. I am flat broke.

Please consider this letter to be a formal request to you to immediately cease all communications with me as per federal law. 15 U.S.C. § 1692c.

If you do not cease further communication I will seek legal action against you and your company.

Signature _____

CC: Federal Trade Commission; Consumer Protection Agency; Department of Business and Professional Regulations; and, Subcommittee on Banking, Credit, and Insurance

APPENDIX C
Motion to Set Aside/Vacate Judgment

APPENDIX C – Motion to Set Aside/Vacate Judgment

_____
(your name)

_____
(address)

_____
(state/zipcode)

_____
(phone number)

IN THE UNITED STATES DISTRICT COURT

FOR THE _____ DISTRICT OF _____
            (Northern,   (State)
         Southern, etc.)

_____ ,
PLAINTIFF (them)

vs.   # _____
                                                            (civil case number)

_____ ,
DEFENDANT (you)

Defendant's: **MOTION TO SET-ASIDE/VACATE JUDGMENT**

COMES NOW _(your name)_ , the defendant in the above numbered civil action, Pro Se, motioning this Court to Set-Aside or Vacate the final judgment entered in this case.

This motion is made in the interest of justice and the defendant will support this motion with both facts and legal arguments as follows:

Page 1 of 5

I. Relevant Facts

1. On or about___(date)___I received a copy of my consumer credit report from the credit bureau(s): (i.e. Equifax, Trans Union, etc.) which listed a default judgment against me from this Court.

2. I contacted the credit bureau(s)and made a formal dispute as to this item being on my credit report but received no relief.

3. After looking further into this judgment on my consumer credit report, came to the realization that___(the Plaintiff)___ had filed a lawsuit against me in this Court and that the Court subsequently entered a default judgment against me and it is this judgment that is now showing up on my credit reports.

4. I know that I never personally received a copy of the lawsuit/complaint against me, nor have I been personally served. So I spoke with all of my family members, neighbors, and people at my job and none of them seem to know anything about it either.

5. This lawsuit/complaint was filed and decided on against me without me having any knowledge about it or any chance to dispute its underlying merits.

II. Points of Law

A default judgment is typically entered whenever the party fails to make an appearance or file an answer or defend the suit against him or her. See e.g. Stafford v. Mesnik, 63 F.3d 1445 (7th Cir. 1995). A defaulted party, however, has not forfeited his jurisdictional challenge. See e.g. Reynolds v. Int'l Amat. Athletic Fed'n, 23 F.3d 1110, 1120 (6th Cir.), cert. den. 130 L. Ed. 2d 338, 115 S.Ct. 423 (1994). The defaulted party may ascribe this failure to flawed or non-existent service of process or other factors that suggest the Court had lacked Personal Jurisdiction over the defendant when it entered its judgment against him. See e.g. United States Aids Funds, Inc. v. Espinosa, 559 U.S. 260, 271, 130 S.Ct. 1367, 176 L. Ed. 2d 158 (2010). This exception to general forfeiture rules recognizes that it is unfair to strip parties of a defense that may very well explain the omission that is potentially the basis for judgment against them. A defaulted party may therefore challenge the district court's exercise of personal jurisdiction in a motion to Set-Aside or Vacate. See e.g. Int'l Harvester v. OSHRC, 628 F.2d 982, 984 (7th Cir. 1980).

Here, the district court never had personal jurisdiction over defendant. And when a court enters a judgment without personal jurisdiction, that judgment is void because the court was powerless to enter it in the first place. See e.g. United States Aids Funds, Inc. at 271. Personal jurisdiction over a defendant represents the power of a court to enter a valid judgment imposing a personal obligation or duty in favor of the plaintiff. See e.g. Viasystems, Inc. v. EBM-Papst St. Georgen GmbH and Co., KG, 646 F.3d 589, 592 (8th Cir. 2011). It can be either specific or general. id. at 593. Specific jurisdiction refers to a defendant's actions within the forum state, while general jurisdiction refers to the power of a state to adjudicate any cause of action involving a particular defendant, regardless of where the cause of action arose. id. Specific personal jurisdiction can be exercised by a federal court in a diversity suit only if authorized by the forum state's long-arm statute and permitted by the Due Process Clause of the Fourteenth Amendment of the Federal Constitution. id. The requirements of the state's long-arm statute and the Due Process Clause present two, independent inquiries that must be addressed as separate issues and the

Page 3 of 5

failure to satisfy either precludes the exercise of specific personal jurisdiction. See e.g. Myers v. Casino Queen, Inc., 689 F.3d 904, 909-10 (8th Cir. 2012).

To satisfy Due Process, a defendant must have sufficient minimum contacts with the forum state such that the assertion of jurisdiction "does not offend traditional notions of fair play and substantial justice." Int'l Shoe Co., v. Washington, 326 U.S. 310, 316, 66 S.Ct. 154, 90 LEd. 95 (1945). Substantial connections between the defendant and the forum state are necessary for the finding of minimum contacts. See e.g. Myers at 911. "[A] defendant's random, fortuitous, or attenuated contacts or on the unilateral activity of plaintiff" is insufficient to establish specific personal jurisdiction. Walden v. Fiore, U.S., 134 S.Ct. 1115, 1123, 188 L. Ed. 2d 12 (2014). Notably, as the record shows, defendant does not have these minimum contacts.

And, as here, where the plaintiff has not effectuated "valid service of process, the district court [is] without jurisdiction of the defendant" id. Armco, Inc. v. Penrod-Stauffer Bldg. Sys., Inc., 733 F.2d 1087, 1089 (4th Cir. 1984).

In order for a court to assert personal jurisdiction over a defendant, "the procedural requirement of service of summons must be satisfied." Omni Capital Int'l v. Rudolf Wolff and Co., 484 U.S. 97, 104, 108 S.Ct. 404, 98 L. Ed. 2d 415 (1987). "Service of summons is the procedure by which a court having venue and jurisdiction of the subject matter of the suit asserts jurisdiction over the person of the party served." Omni Capital Int'l, at 104. "Absent waiver or consent, a failure to obtain proper service on the defendant deprives the court of personal jurisdiction over the defendant." Koehler v. Dodwell, 152 F.3d 304, 306-07 (4th Cir. 1998).

Page 4 of 5

III. Request for Relief

The court was without personal jurisdiction over the defendant when it had entered its default judgment. Defendant neither had the minimum contacts with the forum state, nor was defendant notified of the suit or properly served as required by the Federal Rules of Civil Procedure and the Federal Constitution. WHEREFORE, defendant respectfully moves this Honorable Court to Set-Aside/Vacate the judgment.

Respectfully submitted this day _____ of _____ 20___

_____

Signature

IV. Certificate of Service and Verification of Facts

I _____(defendant)_____ hereby certify under penalty of perjury that I (defendant) have served a true and correct copy of the foregoing on the plaintiff via first class, postage prepaid mail.

And, I swear/affirm under penalty of perjury that facts presented in this foregoing motion are true and correct to the best of my ability.

_____   _____

Signature   Date

CC: Plaintiff
      Clerk of Court
      Personal Record

Page 5 of 5

APPENDIX D
Business Plan Outline

Business Plan Outline

COVER SHEET – Name of business, address of business, your name, date of document.

EXECUTIVE SUMMARY – One or two pages long. Very brief statement covering information listed below. Just state the facts, no citations or references. A quick overview of the entire business and what you want:

    i.   Overview of business

    ii.   Description of product or service

    iii.   Objectives of business

    iv.   The opportunity or strategy

    v.   The target market and projection

    vi.   The competitive advantages

    vii.   Key management people

    viii. Products/Services

    ix.   Financial info

TABLE OF CONTENTS – List key sections and page numbers.
STATEMENT OF OBJECTIVES

    i.   Purpose of product/service – advantages

    ii.   Long range objectives – listed by priority

iii. Personal qualifications – why you feel that you are capable of succeeding in this venture

MANUFACTURING (only if you do your own)

i. Where will it be done?

ii. What size and type of facility?

iii. What lead times will be needed to meet first delivery?

iv. How will it be done?

v. What raw materials will be needed?

vi. What type of labor force will be needed?

vii. Production capacity

viii. Quality control, i.e. warranties, customer service, risk, i.e. toxic material, dangerous environment and the pertinent regulations that will affect it

THE ORGANIZATION

i. Organizational chart

ii. Relevant bio on you and your qualifications

iii. Key positions – top through middle management

iv. Investors?

v. Compensation plans, salary, options, etc.

vi.   Names and biographies of key people (use resumes and exhibits in the Appendix)

vii.   Name and contact info of business attorney, C.P.A., consultants, specialists, experts, etc.

PRICE STRATEGY

i.   Competition's pricing

ii.   Pricing for prestige

iii.   Pricing for image

iv.   Pricing for entry

v.   Buying factors – buyer, retailer, wholesaler

vi.   Is a low price the best way?

PROMOTION

i.   Promotion philosophy

ii.   Promotional plan

iii.   Sales strategy

iv.   Budget for each item

v.   Sample ads in Appendices and Exhibit section

vi.   Advertising and marketing strategy

APPENDIX E
Relevant Parts of
Credit Statute
with Notes

Title 15 of the United States Code: § 1643. Liability of holder of credit card

(a) Limits on liability.

> (1) A cardholder shall be liable for the unauthorized use of a credit card only if

>> (A) the card is an accepted credit card;

>> (B) the liability is not in excess of $50;

>> (C) the card issuer gives adequate notice to the cardholder of the potential liability;

>> (D) the card issuer has provided the cardholder with a description of a means by which the card issuer may be notified of loss or theft of the card, which description may be provided on the face or reverse side of the statement required by section 127(b) [15 USCS § 1637(b)] or on a separate notice accompanying such statement;

>> (E) the unauthorized use occurs before the card issuer has been notified that an unauthorized use of the credit card has occurred or may occur as the result of loss, theft, or otherwise; and

(F) the card issuer has provided a method whereby the user of such card can be identified as the person authorized to use it.

(2) For purposes of this section, a card issuer has been notified when such steps as may be reasonably required in the ordinary course of business to provide the card issuer with the pertinent information have been taken, whether or not any particular officer, employee, or agent of the card issuer does in fact receive such information.

(b) Burden of proof. In any action by a card issuer to enforce liability for the use of a credit card, the burden of proof is upon the card issuer to show that the use was authorized or, if the use was unauthorized, then the burden of proof is upon the card issuer to show that the conditions of liability for the unauthorized use of a credit card, as set forth in subsection (a), have been met.

(c) Liability imposed by other laws or by agreement with issuer. Nothing in this section imposes liability upon a cardholder for the unauthorized use of a credit card in excess of his liability for such use under other applicable law or under any agreement with the card issuer.

(d) Exclusiveness of liability. Except as provided in this section, a cardholder incurs no liability from the unauthorized use of a credit card.

Title 15 of the United States Code: § 1666. Correction of billing errors

(a) Written notice by obligor to creditor; time for and contents of notice; procedure upon receipt of notice by creditor. If a creditor, within sixty days after having transmitted to an obligor a statement of the obligor's account in connection with an extension of consumer credit, receives at the address disclosed under section 127(b)(10) [15 USCS § 1637(b)(10)] a written notice (other than notice on a payment stub of other payment medium supplied by the creditor if the creditor so stipulates with the disclosure required under section 127(a)(7)}[15 USCS § l637(a)(7)]) from the obligor in which the obligor

> (1) sets forth or otherwise enables the creditor to identify the name and account number (if any) of the obligor,
>
> (2) indicates the obligor's belief that the statement contains a billing error and the amount of such billing error, and
>
> (3) sets forth the reasons for the obligor's belief (to the extent applicable) that the statement contains a billing error,

the creditor shall, unless the obligor has, after giving such written notice and before the expiration of the time limits herein specified, agreed that the statement was correct

> (A) not later than thirty days after the receipt of the notice, send a written acknowledgment thereof to the obligor,

unless the action required in subparagraph (B) is taken within such thirty-day period, and

(B) not later than two complete billing cycles of the creditor (in no event later than ninety days) after the receipt of the notice and prior to taking any action to collect the amount, or any part thereof, indicated by the obligor under paragraph (2) either

(i) make appropriate corrections in the account of the obligor, including the crediting of any finance charges on amounts erroneously billed, and transmit to the obligor a notification of such corrections and the creditor's explanation of any change in the amount indicated by the obligor under paragraph (2) and, if any such change is made and the obligor so requests, copies of documentary evidence of the obligor's indebtedness; or

(ii) send a written explanation or clarification to the obligor, after having conducted an investigation, setting forth to the extent applicable the reasons why the creditor believes the account of the obligor was correctly shown in the statement and, upon request of the obligor, provide copies of documentary evidence of the obligor's indebtedness. In the case of a billing error where the obligor alleges that the creditor's billing statement reflects goods not delivered to the obligor or his designee in accordance with the agreement made at the time of the transaction, a creditor may not construe such amount to be correctly shown unless he determines that such goods were actually delivered, mailed, or otherwise sent to the obligor and provides the obligor with a statement of such determination.

After complying with the provisions of this subsection with respect to an alleged billing error, a creditor has no further responsibility under this section if the obligor continues to make substantially the same allegation with respect to such error.

(b) Billing error. For the purpose of this section, a "billing error" consists of any of the following:

(1) A reflection on a statement of an extension of credit which was not made to the obligor or, if made, was not in the amount reflected on such statement.

(2) A reflection on a statement of an extension of credit for which the obligor requests additional clarification including documentary evidence thereof.

(3) A reflection on a statement of goods or services not accepted by the obligor or his designee or not delivered to the obligor or his designee in accordance with the agreement made at the time of a transaction.

(4) The creditor's failure to reflect properly on a statement a payment made by the obligor or a credit issued to the obligor.

(5) A computation error or similar error of an accounting nature of the creditor on a statement.

(6) Failure to transmit the statement required under section 127(b) of this Act [15 USCS § 1637(b)] to the last

address of the obligor which has been disclosed to the creditor, unless that address was furnished less than twenty days before the end of the billing cycle for which the statement is required.

(7) Any other error described in regulations of the Bureau.

(c) Action by creditor to collect amount or any part thereof regarded by obligor to be a billing error. For the purposes of this section, "action to collect the amount, or any part thereof, indicated by an obligor under paragraph (2)" does not include the sending of statements of account, which may include finance charges on amounts in dispute, to the obligor following written notice from the obligor as specified under subsection (a), if

(1) the obligor's account is not restricted or closed because of the failure of the obligor to pay the amount indicated under paragraph (2) of subsection (a), and

(2) the creditor indicates the payment of such amount is not required pending the creditor's compliance with this section.

Nothing in this section shall be construed to prohibit any action by a creditor to collect any amount which has not been indicated by the obligor to contain a billing error.

(d) Restricting or closing by creditor of account regarded by obligor as containing a billing error. Pursuant to regulations of the Bureau, a creditor operating an open end consumer credit plan may not, prior to the sending of the written explanation or clarification required under paragraph (B)(ii), restrict or close an account with respect to which the obligor has indicated pursuant to subsection (a) that he believes such account to contain a billing error solely because of the obligor's failure to pay the amount indicated to be in error. Nothing in this subsection shall be deemed to prohibit a creditor from applying against the credit limit on the obligor's account the amount indicated to be in error.

(e) Effect of noncompliance with requirements by creditor. Any creditor who fails to comply with the requirements of this section or section 162 [15 USCS § 1666a] forfeits any right to collect from the obligor the amount indicated by the obligor under paragraph (2) of subsection (a) of this section, and any finance charges thereon, except that the amount required to be forfeited under this subsection may not exceed $50.

Title 15 of the United States Code: § 1666a. Regulation of credit reports

(a) **Reports by creditor on obligor's failure to pay amount regarded as billing error.** After receiving a notice from an obligor as provided in section 161(a) [15 USCS § 1666(a)], a creditor or his agent may not directly or indirectly threaten to report to any person adversely on the obligor's credit rating or credit standing because of the obligor's failure to pay the amount indicated by the obligor under section 161(a)(2) [15 USCS § 1666(a)(2)], and such amount may not be reported as delinquent to any third party until the creditor has met the requirements of section 161 [15 USCS § 1666] and has allowed the obligor the same number of days (not less than ten) thereafter to make payment as is provided under the credit agreement with the obligor for the payment of undisputed amounts.

(b) **Reports by creditor on delinquent amounts in dispute; notification of obligor of parties notified of delinquency.** If a creditor receives a further 'Written notice from an obligor that an amount is still in dispute within the time allowed for payment under subsection (a) of this section, a creditor may not report to any third party that the amount of the obligor is delinquent because the obligor has failed to pay an amount which he has indicated under section 161(a)(2) [15 USCS § 1666(a)(2)], unless the creditor also reports that the amount is in dispute and, at the same time, notifies the obligor of the name and address of each party to whom the creditor is reporting information concerning the delinquency.

(c) **Reports by creditor of subsequent resolution of delinquent amounts.** A creditor shall report any subsequent resolution of any delinquencies reported pursuant to subsection (b) to the parties to whom such delinquencies were initially reported.

Title 15 of the United States Code: § 1681i. Procedure in case of disputed accuracy

(a) Reinvestigations of disputed information.

(1) Reinvestigation required.

(A) In general. Subject to subsection (f), if the completeness or accuracy of any item of information contained in a consumer's file at a consumer reporting agency is disputed by the consumer and the consumer notifies the agency directly, or indirectly through a reseller, of such dispute, the agency shall, free of charge, conduct a reasonable reinvestigation to determine whether the disputed information is inaccurate and record the current status of the disputed information, or delete the item from the file in accordance with paragraph (5), before the end of the 30-day period beginning on the date on. Which the agency receives the notice of the dispute from the consumer or reseller.

(B) Extension of period to reinvestigate. Except as provided in subparagraph (C), the 30-day period described in subparagraph (A) may be extended for not more than 15 additional days if the consumer reporting agency receives information from the consumer during that 30-day period that is relevant to the reinvestigation.

(C) Limitations on extension of period to reinvestigate. Subparagraph (B) shall not apply to any reinvestigation in which, during the 30-day period described in subparagraph (A), the information that is the subject of the reinvestigation is found to be inaccurate or incomplete or the consumer reporting agency determines that the information cannot be verified.

(2) Prompt notice of dispute to furnisher of information.

(A) In general. Before the expiration of the 5-business-day period beginning on the date on which a consumer reporting agency receives notice of a dispute from any consumer or a reseller in accordance with paragraph (1), the agency shall provide notification of the dispute to any person who provided any item of information in dispute, at the address and in the manner established with the person. The notice shall include all relevant information regarding the dispute that the agency has received from the consumer or reseller.

(B) Provision of other information. The consumer reporting agency shall promptly provide to the person who provided the information in dispute all relevant information regarding the dispute that is received by the agency from the consumer or the reseller after the period referred to in subparagraph (A) and before the end of the period referred to in paragraph (1)(A).

(3) Determination that dispute is frivolous or irrelevant.

The Underground Credit Builder's Handbook

(A) In general. Notwithstanding paragraph (1), a consumer reporting agency may terminate a reinvestigation of information disputed by a consumer under that paragraph if the agency reasonably determines that the dispute by the consumer is frivolous or irrelevant, including by reason of a failure by a consumer to provide sufficient information to investigate the disputed information.

(B) Notice of determination. Upon making any determination in accordance with subparagraph (A) that a dispute is frivolous or irrelevant, a consumer reporting agency shall notify the consumer of such determination not later than 5 business days after making such determination by mail or, if authorized by the consumer for that purpose, by any other means available to the agency.

(C) Contents of notice. A notice under subparagraph (B) shall include

(i) the reasons for the determination under subparagraph (A); and

(ii) identification of any information required to investigate the disputed information, which may consist of a standardized form describing the general nature of such information.

(4) Consideration of consumer information. In conducting any reinvestigation under paragraph (1) with respect to disputed information in the file of any consumer, the

106

consumer reporting agency shall review and consider all relevant information submitted by the consumer in the period described in paragraph (1)(A) with respect to such disputed information.

(5) Treatment of inaccurate or unverifiable information.

(A) In general. If, after any reinvestigation under paragraph (1) of any information disputed by a consumer, an item of the information is found to be inaccurate or incomplete or cannot be verified, the consumer reporting agency shall

(i) promptly delete that item of information from the file of the consumer, or modify that item of information, as appropriate, based on the results of the reinvestigation; and

(ii) promptly notify the furnisher of that information that the information has been modified or deleted from the file of the consumer.

(B) Requirements relating to reinsertion of previously deleted material.

(i) Certification of accuracy of information. If any information is deleted from a consumer's file pursuant to subparagraph (A), the information may not be reinserted in the file by the consumer reporting agency unless the person who furnishes the information certifies that the information is complete and accurate.

(ii) Notice to consumer. If any information that has been deleted from a consumer's file pursuant to subparagraph (A) is reinserted in the file, the consumer reporting agency shall notify the consumer of the reinsertion in writing not later than 5 business days after the reinsertion or, if authorized by the consumer for that purpose, by any other means available to the agency.

(iii) Additional information. As part of, or in addition to, the notice under clause (ii), a consumer reporting agency shall provide to a consumer in writing not later than 5 business days after the date of the reinsertion

(I) a statement that the disputed information has been reinserted;

(II) the business name and address of any furnisher of information contacted and the telephone number of such furnisher, if reasonably available, or of any furnisher of information that contacted the consumer reporting agency, in connection with the reinsertion of such information; and

(III) a notice that the consumer has the right to add a statement to the consumer's file disputing the accuracy or completeness of the disputed information.

(C) Procedures to prevent reappearance. A consumer reporting agency shall maintain reasonable procedures designed to prevent the reappearance in a consumer's file, and in consumer reports on the consumer, of information that is deleted pursuant to this paragraph (other than information that is reinserted in accordance with subparagraph (B)(i)).

(D) Automated reinvestigation system. Any consumer reporting agency that compiles and maintains files on consumers on a nationwide basis shall implement an automated system through which furnishers of information to that consumer reporting agency may report the results of a reinvestigation that finds incomplete or inaccurate information in a consumer's file to other such consumer reporting agencies.

(6) Notice of results of reinvestigation.

(A) In general. A consumer reporting agency shall provide written notice to a consumer of the results of a reinvestigation under this subsection not later than 5 business days after the completion of the reinvestigation, by mail or, if authorized by the consumer for that purpose, by other means available to the agency.

(B) Contents. As part of, or in addition to, the notice under subparagraph (A), a consumer reporting agency shall provide to a consumer in writing before the expiration of the 5-day period referred to in subparagraph (A)

(i) a statement that the reinvestigation is completed;

(ii) a consumer report that is based upon the consumer's file as that file is revised as a result of the reinvestigation;

(iii) a notice that, if requested by the consumer, a description of the procedure used to determine the accuracy and completeness of the information shall be provided to the consumer by the agency, including the business name and address of any furnisher of information contacted in connection with such information and the telephone number of such furnisher, if reasonably available;

(iv) a notice that the consumer has the right to add a statement to the consumer's file disputing the accuracy or completeness of the information; and

(v) a notice that the consumer has the right to request under subsection (d) that the consumer reporting agency furnish notifications under that subsection.

(7) Description of reinvestigation procedure. A consumer reporting agency shall provide to a consumer a description referred to in paragraph (6)(B)(iii) by not later than 15 days after receiving a request from the consumer for that description.

(8) Expedited dispute resolution. If a dispute regarding an item of information in a consumer's file at a consumer reporting agency is resolved in accordance with paragraph

(5)(A) by the deletion of the disputed information by not later than 3 business days after the date on which the agency receives notice of the dispute from the consumer in accordance with paragraph (I)(A), then the agency shall not be required to comply with paragraphs (2), (6), and (7) with respect to that dispute if the agency

(A) provides prompt notice of the deletion to the consumer by telephone;

(B) includes in that notice, or in a written notice that accompanies a confirmation and consumer report provided in accordance with subparagraph (C), a statement of the consumer's right to request under subsection (d) that the agency furnish notifications under that subsection; and

(C) provides written confirmation of the deletion and a copy of a consumer report on the consumer that is based on the consumer's file after the deletion, not later than 5 business days after making the deletion.

(b) **Statement of dispute.** If the reinvestigation does not resolve the dispute, the consumer may file a brief statement setting forth the nature of the dispute. The consumer reporting agency may limit such statements to not more than one hundred words if it provides the consumer with assistance in writing a clear summary of the dispute.

(c) **Notification of consumer dispute in subsequent consumer reports.** Whenever a statement of a dispute is filed, unless there is reasonable grounds to believe that it is frivolous or irrelevant, the consumer reporting agency shall, in any subsequent consumer report containing the information in question, clearly note that it is disputed by the consumer and provide either the consumer's statement or a clear and accurate codification or summary thereof.

(d) **Notification of deletion of disputed information.** Following any deletion of information which is found to be inaccurate or whose accuracy can no longer be verified or any notation as to disputed information, the consumer reporting agency shall, at the request of the consumer, furnish notification that the item has been deleted or the statement, codification or summary pursuant to subsection (b) or (c) to any person specifically designated by the consumer who has within two years prior thereto received a consumer report for employment purposes, or within six months prior thereto received a consumer report for any other purpose, which contained the deleted or disputed information.

(e) Treatment of complaints and report to Congress.

(1) In general. The Commission shall

(A) compile all complaints that it receives that a file of a consumer that is maintained by a consumer reporting agency described in section 603(p) [15 uses § 1681a(p)] contains incomplete or inaccurate information, with respect to which, the consumer appears to have disputed the completeness or accuracy with the consumer reporting agency or otherwise utilized the procedures provided by subsection (a); and

(B) transmit each such complaint to each consumer reporting agency involved.

(2) Exclusion. Complaints received or obtained by the Bureau pursuant to its investigative authority under the Consumer Financial Protection Act of 2010 shall not be subject to paragraph (1).

(3) Agency responsibilities. Each consumer reporting agency described in section 603(p) [15 USCS § 1681a(p)] that receives a complaint transmitted by the Bureau pursuant to paragraph (1) shall

(A) review each such complaint to determine whether all legal obligations imposed on the consumer reporting agency under this title [15 uses §§ 1681 et seq.] (including any obligation imposed by an applicable court or administrative order) have been met with respect to the subject matter of the complaint;

(B) provide reports on a regular basis to the Bureau regarding the determinations of and actions taken by the consumer reporting agency, if any, in connection with its review of such complaints; and

(C) maintain, for a reasonable time period, records regarding the disposition of each such complaint that is sufficient to demonstrate compliance with this subsection.

(4) Rulemaking authority. The Commission may prescribe regulations, as appropriate to implement this subsection.

(5) Annual report. The Commission shall submit to the Committee on Banking, Housing, and Urban Affairs of the Senate and the Committee on Financial Services of the

House of Representatives an annual report regarding information gathered by the Bureau under this subsection.

(f) Reinvestigation requirement applicable to resellers.

(1) Exemption from general reinvestigation requirement. Except as provided in paragraph (2), a reseller shall be exempt from the requirements of this section.

(2) Action required upon receiving notice of a dispute. If a reseller receives a notice from a consumer of a dispute concerning the completeness or accuracy of any item of information contained in a consumer report on such consumer produced by the reseller, the reseller shall, within 5 business days of receiving the notice, and free of charge.

(A) determine whether the item of information is incomplete or inaccurate as a result of an act or omission of the reseller; and

(B) if

(i) the reseller determines that the item of information is incomplete or inaccurate as a result of an act or omission of the reseller, not later than 20 days after receiving the notice, correct the information in the consumer report or delete it; or

(ii) if the reseller determines that the item of information is not incomplete or inaccurate as a result of an act or omission of the reseller, convey the notice of the dispute, together with all relevant information provided by the consumer, to each consumer reporting agency that provided the reseller with the information that is the subject of the dispute, using an address or a notification mechanism specified by the consumer reporting agency for such notices.

(3) Responsibility of consumer reporting agency to notify consumer through reseller. Upon the completion of a reinvestigation under this section of a dispute concerning the completeness or accuracy of any information in the file of a consumer by a consumer reporting agency that received notice of the dispute from a reseller under paragraph (2)

(A) the notice by the consumer reporting agency under paragraph (6), (7), or (8) of subsection (a) shall be provided to the reseller in lieu of the consumer; and

(B) the reseller shall immediately reconvey such notice to the consumer, including any notice of a deletion by telephone in the manner required under paragraph (8)(A).

(4) Reseller reinvestigations. No provision of this subsection shall be construed as prohibiting a reseller from conducting a reinvestigation of a consumer dispute directly.

Title 15 of the United States Code: § 1692d. Harassment or abuse

A debt collector may not engage in any conduct the natural consequence of which is to harass, oppress, or abuse any person in connection with the collection of a debt. Without limiting the general application of the foregoing, the following conduct a violation of this section:

(1) The use or threat of use of violence or other criminal means to harm the physical person, reputation, or property of any person.

(2) The use of obscene or profane language or language the natural consequence of which is to abuse the hearer or reader.

(3) The publication of a list of consumers who allegedly refuse to pay debts, except to a consumer reporting agency or to persons meeting the requirements of section 603(f) or 604(3) [604(a)(3)] of this Act [15 USCS § l681a(f) or 1681b(a)(3)]

(4)The advertisement for sale of any debt to coerce payment of the debt.

(5) Causing a telephone to ring or engaging any person in telephone conversation repeatedly or continuously with intent to annoy, abuse, or harass any person at the called number.

(6) Except as provided in section 804 [15 USCS § 1692b], the placement of telephone calls without meaningful disclosure of the caller's identity.

Title 15 of the United States Code: § 1692 Unfair practices

A debt collector may not use unfair or unconscionable means to collect or attempt to collect any debt. Without limiting the general application of the foregoing, the following conduct is a violation of this section:

(1) The collection of any amount (including any interest, fee, charge, or expense incidental to the principal obligation) unless such amount is expressly authorized by the agreement creating the debt or permitted by law.

(2) The acceptance by a debt collector from any person of a check or other payment instrument postdated by more than five days unless such person is notified in writing of the debt collector's intent to deposit such check or instrument not more than ten nor less than three business days prior to such deposit.

(3) The solicitation by a debt collector of any postdated check or other postdated payment instrument for the purpose of threatening or instituting criminal prosecution.

(4) Depositing or threatening to deposit any postdated check or other postdated payment instrument prior to the date on such check or instrument.

(5) Causing charges to be made to any person for communications by concealment of the true purpose of the communication. Such charges include, but are not limited to, collect telephone calls and telegram fees.

(6) Taking or threatening to take any nonjudicial action to effect dispossession or disablement of property if

(A) there is no present right to possession of the property claimed as collateral through an enforceable security interest;

(B) there is no present intention to take possession of the property; or

(C) the property is exempt by law from such dispossession or disablement.

(7) Communicating with a consumer regarding a debt by post card.

(8) Using any language or symbol, other than the debt collector's address, on any envelope when communicating with a consumer by use of the mails or by telegram, except that a debt collector may use his business name if such name does not indicate that he is in the debt collection business.

Title 15 of the United States Code: § 1692g. Validation of debts

(a) **Notice of debt: contents.** Within five days after the initial communication with a consumer in connection with the collection of any debt, a debt collector shall, unless the following information is contained in the initial communication or the consumer has paid the debt, send the consumer a written notice containing

> (1) the amount of the debt;

> (2) the name of the creditor to whom the debt is owed;

> (3) a statement that unless the consumer, within thirty days after receipt of the notice, disputes the validity of the debt, or any portion thereof, the debt will be assumed to be valid by the debt collector;

> (4) a statement that if the consumer notifies the debt collector in writing within the thirty-day period that the debt, or any portion thereof, is disputed, the debt collector will obtain verification of the debt or a copy of a judgment against the consumer and a copy of such verification or judgment will be mailed to the consumer by the debt collector; and

> (5) a statement that, upon the consumer's written request within the thirty-day period, the debt collector will provide the consumer with the name and address of the original creditor, if different from the current creditor.

(b) **Disputed debts**. If the consumer notifies the debt collector in writing within the thirty-day period described in subsection (a) that the debt, or any portion thereof, is disputed, or that the consumer requests the name and address of the original creditor, the debt collector shall cease collection of the debt, or any disputed portion thereof, until the debt collector obtains verification of the debt or a copy of a judgment, or the name and address of the original creditor, and a copy of such verification or judgment, or name and address of the original creditor, is mailed to the consumer by the debt collector. Collection activities and communications that do not otherwise violate this title may continue during the 30-day period referred to in subsection (a) unless the consumer has notified the debt collector in writing that the debt, or any portion of the debt, is disputed or that the consumer requests the name and address of the original creditor. Any collection activities and communication during the 30-day period may not overshadow or be inconsistent with the disclosure of the consumer's right to dispute the debt or request the name and address of the original creditor.

(c) **Admission of liability.** The failure of a consumer to dispute the validity of a debt under this section may not be construed by any court as an admission of liability by the consumer.

(d) **Legal pleadings.** A communication in the form of a formal pleading in a civil action shall not be treated as an initial communication for purposes of subsection (a).

(e) **Notice provisions.** The sending or delivery of any form or notice which does not relate to the collection of a debt and is expressly required by the Internal Revenue Code of 1986 [26 USCS §§ 1 et seq.], title V of Gramm-Leach-Bliley Act [15 USCS §§ 6801 et seq.], or any provision of Federal or State law relating to notice of data security breach or privacy, or any regulation prescribed under any such provision of law, shall not be treated as an initial communication in connection with debt collection for purposes of this section.

Notes on the Fair Credit Reporting Act, 15 U.S.C. § 1681, et seq.

The Fair Credit Reporting Act "was enacted to require that consumer reporting agencies adopt reasonable procedures for meeting the needs of commerce for consumer credit in a manner which is fair and equitable to the consumer, with regard to the confidentiality, accuracy, relevancy, and proper utilization of such information." id. Chipka v. Bank of Am., 355 F. App'x 380, 382 (11th Cir. 2009)(citing 15 U.S.C. § 1681[b]). Under the FCRA, upon receiving notice of a dispute, furnishers of information must conduct an investigation regarding the disputed information. 15 U.S.S. § 1681s-2(b)(1); Chipka, 355 F. App'x at 383 ("the FCRA also imposes certain responsibilities on persons who furnish information to consumer reporting agencies"). Title 15, United States Code, Section 1681s-2(b)(2) requires a furnisher of information to complete all investigations and obligations imposed by 15 U.S.S. § 1681s-2(b)(1) within the time that is prescribed by 15 U.S.C. § 1681i(a)(1), which is thirty days from the date the credit bureau receives notice of the dispute. 15 U.S.C. § 1681i(a)(1). Any person who fails to comply with these requirements may be subject to liability based on 15 U.S.C. §§ 1681n (willful noncompliance) and 1681o (negligent non- compliance).

The statutory language of Sections 1681s-2(b)(2) and 1681i(a)(1)(A) clearly provides for a deadline by which a furnisher of information must complete its reinvestigation duties: thirty days from a consumer reporting agency's receipt of notice of the dispute. Indeed, Section 1681s-2(b)(2) is titled "Deadline."

A deadline is a "time limit" – The American Heritage Dictionary of the English Language (4th ed. 2000). A "limit," in turn, is "[t]he point, edge, or line beyond which something cannot or may not proceed, [a] confining or restricting object, agent, or influence" – The American Heritage Dictionary of the English Language (4th ed. 2000). In other words, under Sections 1681s-2(b)(2) and 1681i(a)(1)(A), the most time that an information furnisher may take to finish its reinvestigation duties is thirty days.

A consumer is entitled to punitive damages when the evidence demonstrates that the consumer reporting agency "willfully failed" to follow the FCRA's requirements. 15 U.S.C. § 1681n. If a consumer reporting agency commits a "willful violation" under either 15 U.S.C. § 1681e(b) or 15 U.S.C. § 1681i, punitive damages may be imposed. Pinner v. Schmidt, 805 F.2d 1258, 1262 (5th Cir. 1886). As explained in Stevenson v. TRW, Inc., 987 F.2d 288 (5th Cir. 1993), "to be found in willful noncompliance, a defendant must have 'knowingly and intentionally committed an act in conscious disregard for the rights of others.' Although malice or evil motive is not necessary to satisfy §1681n, there must have been a willful violation." id. at 294 (citations omitted). For example, at least one court has found that a consumer reporting agency's haphazardness in verifying consumer credit information was sufficient to support an award of punitive damages. See Collins v. Retail Credit Co., 410 F. Supp. 924, 932 and 933-34 (E.D. Mich. 1976)(finding that the issue of punitive damages was properly submitted to the jury where the evidence demonstrated "willful and reckless wrongdoing"; the consumer reporting agency's "procedures and techniques in investigating, disclosing, and reporting were inexact and indicated a reckless disregard and indifference for the accuracy of the accusations contained in the report.").

Notes on the Fair Debt Collection Practices Act, 15 U.S.C. § 1692, et seq.

The Fair Debt Collection Act was enacted to eliminate abusive debt collection practices, to ensure that debt collectors who abstain from such practices are not competitively disadvantaged, and to promote consistent state action to protect consumers. 15 U.S.C. § 1692(e). The act regulates interactions between consumer debtors and "debt collector[s]," defined to include any person who "regularly collects debts owed or due or asserted to be owed or due another." §§ 1692 a(5), (6). Among other things, the act prohibits debt collectors from making false representations as to a debt's character, amount, or legal status, § 1692 e(2)(A); communicating with consumers at an "unusual time or place" likely to be inconvenient to the consumer, § 1692c(a)(1); or using obscene or profane language or violence or the threat thereof; §§ 1692(d)(1), (2). See, e.g. §§ 1692b-1692j; Heintz v. Jenkins, 514 U.S. 291, 292-293, 115 S.Ct. 1489, 131 L.Ed. 2d 395 (1995).

The FDCPA requires validation of a disputed debt by debt collectors. 15 U.S.C. § 1692g. If a consumer requests the identity of the original creditor within the thirty-day period, "the debt collector will provide the consumer with the name and address of the original creditor, if different from the current creditor." 15 U.S.C. § 1692g(a)(5). The FDCPA is enforced through administrative action and private lawsuits.

With some exceptions not relevant here, violations of the FDCPA are deemed to be unfair or deceptive acts or practices under the Federal Trade Commission Act, 15 U.S.C. § 41 et seq., and are enforced by the Federal Trade Commission. See § 1692. As a result, a debt collector who acts with "actual knowledge or knowledge fairly implied on the basis of objective circumstances that such act is [prohibitive under the FDCPA]" is subject to civil penalties of up to $16,000 per day. §§ 45(m)(1)(A), (C); 74 Fed. Reg. 858 (2009)(amending 16 C.F.R. § 1.98 (d))

According to the FTC, the consumer report user's adverse-action letter "should provide the name and address of the consumer reporting agency from which it obtained the consumer report, even if that agency obtained all or part of the report from another agency." – FTC Commentary on the Fair Credit Reporting Act, 16 C.F.R. pt. 600, App. § 615 P13. And it is thus advised that the same information be included in dispute letters under the FDCPA.

The FDCPA also provides that "any debt collector who fails to comply with any provision of the act with respect to any person is liable to such person." 15 U.S.C. § 1692k(a). Successful plaintiffs are entitled to "actual damage[s]," plus costs and "a reasonable attorney's fee as determined by the court." id. A court may also award "additional damages," subject to a statutory cap of $1,000 for individual actions, or, for class actions, "the lesser of $500,000 or 1 per centum of the net worth of the debt collector." § 1692k(a)(2). In awarding additional damages, the court must consider "the frequency and persistence of [the debt collector's] noncompliance," "the nature of such noncompliance," and "the extent to which such noncompliance was intentional." § 1693k(b).

APPENDIX F
Identity Theft
Complaint form

Average time to complete: 10 minutes ▶

Identity Theft Victim's Complaint and Affidavit

A voluntary form for filing a report with law enforcement, and disputes with credit reporting agencies and creditors about identity theft-related problems. Visit identitytheft.gov to use a secure online version that you can print for your records.

Before completing this form:
1. Place a fraud alert on your credit reports, and review the reports for signs of fraud.
2. Close the accounts that you know, or believe, have been tampered with or opened fraudulently.

About You *(the victim)*
Now

(1) My full legal name: _____
     First   Middle   Last   Suffix

(2) My date of birth: _____
     mm/dd/yyyy

(3) My Social Security number: _____-_____-_____

(4) My driver's license: _____ _____
     State   Number

(5) My current street address:

     _____
     Number & Street Name   Apartment, Suite, etc.

     _____
     City   State   Zip Code   Country

(6) I have lived at this address since _____
     mm/yyyy

(7) My daytime phone: (____)_____

     My evening phone: (____)_____

     My email: _____

> Leave (3) blank until you provide this form to someone with a legitimate business need, like when you are filing your report at the police station or sending the form to a credit reporting agency to correct your credit report.

At the Time of the Fraud

(8) My full legal name was: _____
     First   Middle   Last   Suffix

(9) My address was: _____
     Number & Street Name   Apartment, Suite, etc.

     _____
     City   State   Zip Code   Country

(10) My daytime phone: (____)_____ My evening phone: (____)_____

     My email: _____

> Skip (8) - (10) if your information has not changed since the fraud.

The Paperwork Reduction Act requires the FTC to display a valid control number (in this case, OMB control #3084-0047) before we can collect – or sponsor the collection of – your information, or require you to provide it.

Victim's Name _____ Phone number (___)_____ Page 2

About You (the victim) (Continued)

Declarations

(11) I ☐ did OR ☐ did not authorize anyone to use my name or personal information to obtain money, credit, loans, goods, or services — or for any other purpose — as described in this report.

(12) I ☐ did OR ☐ did not receive any money, goods, services, or other benefit as a result of the events described in this report.

(13) I ☐ am OR ☐ am not willing to work with law enforcement if charges are brought against the person(s) who committed the fraud.

About the Fraud

(14) I believe the following person used my information or identification documents to open new accounts, use my existing accounts, or commit other fraud.

(14): Enter what you know about anyone you believe was involved (even if you don't have complete information).

Name: _____
First   Middle   Last   Suffix

Address: _____
Number & Street Name   Apartment, Suite, etc.

_____
City   State   Zip Code   Country

Phone Numbers: (___)_____ (___)_____

Additional information about this person: _____
_____
_____
_____
_____
_____
_____
_____
_____
_____
_____

APPENDIX F – Identity Theft Complaint form

Victim's Name _____ *Phone number (___)_____* *Page 3*

(15) Additional information about the crime (for example, how the identity thief gained access to your information or which documents or information were used):

_____

_____

_____

(14) and (15): Attach additional sheets as needed.

_____

_____

_____

_____

Documentation

(16) I can verify my identity with these documents:

☐ A valid government-issued photo identification card (for example, my driver's license, state-issued ID card, or my passport).
If you are under 16 and don't have a photo-ID, a copy of your birth certificate or a copy of your official school record showing your enrollment and legal address is acceptable.

☐ Proof of residency during the time the disputed charges occurred, the loan was made, or the other event took place (for example, a copy of a rental/lease agreement in my name, a utility bill, or an insurance bill).

(16): Reminder: Attach copies of your identity documents when sending this form to creditors and credit reporting agencies.

About the Information or Accounts

(17) The following personal information (like my name, address, Social Security number, or date of birth) in my credit report is inaccurate as a result of this identity theft:

(A) _____

(B) _____

(C) _____

(18) Credit inquiries from these companies appear on my credit report as a result of this identity theft:

Company Name: _____

Company Name: _____

Company Name: _____

(19)   Below are details about the different frauds committed using my personal information.

Name of Institution   Contact Person   Phone   Extension

Account Number   Routing Number   Affected Check Number(s)

Account Type: ☐ Credit   ☐ Bank   ☐ Phone/Utilities   ☐ Loan
              ☐ Government Benefits   ☐ Internet or Email   ☐ Other

Select ONE:
    ☐ This account was opened fraudulently.
    ☐ This was an existing account that someone tampered with.

Date Opened or Misused (mm/yyyy)   Date Discovered (mm/yyyy)   Total Amount Obtained ($)

Name of Institution   Contact Person   Phone   Extension

Account Number   Routing Number   Affected Check Number(s)

Account Type: ☐ Credit   ☐ Bank   ☐ Phone/Utilities   ☐ Loan
              ☐ Government Benefits   ☐ Internet or Email   ☐ Other

Select ONE:
    ☐ This account was opened fraudulently.
    ☐ This was an existing account that someone tampered with.

Date Opened or Misused (mm/yyyy)   Date Discovered (mm/yyyy)   Total Amount Obtained ($)

Name of Institution   Contact Person   Phone   Extension

Account Number   Routing Number   Affected Check Number(s)

Account Type: ☐ Credit   ☐ Bank   ☐ Phone/Utilities   ☐ Loan
              ☐ Government Benefits   ☐ Internet or Email   ☐ Other

Select ONE:
    ☐ This account was opened fraudulently.
    ☐ This was an existing account that someone tampered with.

Date Opened or Misused (mm/yyyy)   Date Discovered (mm/yyyy)   Total Amount Obtained ($)

---

(19):
If there were more than three frauds, copy this page blank, and attach as many additional copies as necessary.

Enter any applicable information that you have, even if it is incomplete or an estimate.

If the thief committed two types of fraud at one company, list the company twice, giving the information about the two frauds separately.

Contact Person: Someone you dealt with, whom an investigator can call about this fraud.

Account Number: The number of the credit or debit card, bank account, loan, or other account that was misused.

Dates: Indicate when the thief began to misuse your information and when you discovered the problem.

Amount Obtained: For instance, the total amount purchased with the card or withdrawn from the account.

APPENDIX F – Identity Theft Complaint form

Victim's Name _____ *Phone number (___)_____* *Page 5*

Your Law Enforcement Report

(20) One way to get a credit reporting agency to quickly block identity theft-related information from appearing on your credit report is to submit a detailed law enforcement report ("Identity Theft Report"). You can obtain an Identity Theft Report by taking this form to your local law enforcement office, along with your supporting documentation. Ask an officer to witness your signature and complete the rest of the information in this section. It's important to get your report number, whether or not you are able to file in person or get a copy of the official law enforcement report. Attach a copy of any confirmation letter or official law enforcement report you receive when sending this form to credit reporting agencies.

(20): Check "I have not..." if you have not yet filed a report with law enforcement or you have chosen not to. Check "I was unable..." if you tried to file a report but law enforcement refused to take it.

Automated report: A law enforcement report filed through an automated system, for example, by telephone, mail, or the Internet, instead of a face-to-face interview with a law enforcement officer.

Select ONE:

☐ I have not filed a law enforcement report.

☐ I was unable to file any law enforcement report.

☐ I filed an automated report with the law enforcement agency listed below.

☐ I filed my report in person with the law enforcement officer and agency listed below.

_____
Law Enforcement Department   State

_____   _____
Report Number   Filing Date (mm/dd/yyyy)

_____   _____
Officer's Name (please print)   Officer's Signature

_____   (___)_____
Badge Number   Phone Number

Did the victim receive a copy of the report from the law enforcement officer?   ☐ Yes OR ☐ No

Victim's FTC complaint number (if available): _____

Victim's Name _____ *Phone number (____)_____* *Page 6*

Signature

As applicable, sign and date *IN THE PRESENCE OF* a law enforcement officer, a notary, or a witness.

(21)   I certify that, to the best of my knowledge and belief, all of the information on and attached to this complaint is true, correct, and complete and made in good faith. I understand that this complaint or the information it contains may be made available to federal, state, and/or local law enforcement agencies for such action within their jurisdiction as they deem appropriate. I understand that knowingly making any false or fraudulent statement or representation to the government may violate federal, state, or local criminal statutes, and may result in a fine, imprisonment, or both.

_____   _____
Signature   Date Signed (mm/dd/yyyy)

Your Affidavit

(22)   If you do not choose to file a report with law enforcement, you may use this form as an Identity Theft Affidavit to prove to each of the companies where the thief misused your information that you are not responsible for the fraud. While many companies accept this affidavit, others require that you submit different forms. Check with each company to see if it accepts this form. You should also check to see if it requires notarization. If so, sign in the presence of a notary. If it does not, please have one witness (non-relative) sign that you completed and signed this Affidavit. If someone has used your Social Security number (SSN) to get a tax refund or a job, or you suspect your SSN has been stolen, alert the IRS using Form 14039 at **www.irs.gov/pub/irs-pdf/f14039.pdf**.

_____
Notary

Witness:

_____   _____
Signature   Printed Name

_____   _____
Date   Telephone Number

134

www.ingramcontent.com/pod-product-compliance
Lightning Source LLC
Chambersburg PA
CBHW060609200326
41521CB00007B/712